Dear Soph,

To celebrate your first communion!

LOTS of love

Susannah xxxx

Boy With a Secret

DayOne

First printed 2016

ISBN 978-1-84625-522-9

Published by Day One Publications
Ryelands Road, Leominster, HR6 8NZ

TEL 01568 613 740 FAX 01568 611 473

email—sales@dayone.co.uk

UK web site—www.dayone.co.uk

Designed by **documen**
Printed by TJ International

Dedication

Dedicated to my grandson—Albert—born just before the publication of this book. (And in memory of his great grandfather and great, great grandfather—who shared his name.)

Chapter one

"I forbid it!" the man said fiercely, lifting himself from his bed as he spoke, only to sink down again when a fit of coughing shook his body.

The two old women in the workshop heard his cry. They paused in their spinning for a moment to glance at the sick man in the next room, his wife and daughter standing anxiously by his side. Then they turned back, picked up their spindles and continued their work, twisting the strands of wool into thread.

"We have very little choice, Timon," his wife replied sadly. "You're too ill to walk and we have no son to carry on the work."

"It will be fine, Father," the girl said eagerly. "I've been to market with you many times and know exactly what to do."

"Most of our workers have gone to find other places to work because we can't pay them," the woman continued, looking into the workshop at the two other women, the stack of unspun wool on one side of them and the bobbins of thread ready to be sold on the other, "and we can't expect Lois and Dorcas to carry on working for nothing."

"I'll be better soon," Timon pleaded. "Please, Lilah, just give me a day or two to recover, then I can take the thread to sell. It's no job for Julianna—it's not safe for a girl to go alone to the market."

"You've been saying that for three weeks," the girl answered sadly. "Please let me go, Father. You need good food if you are going to get strong."

"We have many bundles of yarn that should fetch a good price at the market," Lilah said, glancing again into the workshop where the balls of wool and thread were stacked up in a huge pile against the wall. "They are no use to us sitting in the workshop. If we could sell some we will be able to buy more wool for the women to spin."

Wearily, the man looked at his wife. "Very well, Lilah," he sighed at last, leaning back against the pillow and closing his eyes. "Do whatever you think best."

Gently Lilah tucked the blanket around her husband and turned to her daughter. "Julianna," she said quietly, handing her a bundle of clothes, "take these and find some that fit you. And fetch me my scissors."

Julianna did as she was told. She took the clothes from her mother and went into the back room. A few minutes later she returned, dressed in a cotton shirt so long that it touched the floor. "This is the shortest one I could find," she said.

"That's alright," her mother replied, smiling sadly at the comical sight of Julianna in her father's shirt. "I'll make it shorter and it will be fine with a leather belt round the waist. Your sandals could belong to either a man or a girl so they're fine."

Lilah quickly set to altering the shirt so that it came just below Julianna's knees. Then they found a goat's hair coat in the workshop. It had belonged to one of their young workers who had left them a year ago to find a better paid job. They had kept it in case he came back for it. It fitted Julianna well. "That will help keep you warm on cold mornings," Lilah said. Then, sighing heavily and holding up the scissors, she looked hard at her daughter. "Julianna," she asked, "are you sure about this?"

Julianna smiled bravely and pulled off the band that held her coiled hair in its place on top of her head. Her hair tumbled around her shoulders in a dark cloud. "It's only hair, Mother," she said, "it will grow again."

There was a groan from the bed as Timon saw what was happening. "No, please. Not her beautiful hair," he whispered, before breaking into another coughing fit. But it was already too late. Piece by piece her fine, dark hair was falling like long threads of silk onto the floor around them.

At last, Lilah put her scissors down. "There," she said, standing back to look at her daughter, biting her lip and rubbing her eyes as she did so.

Julianna put her hands to her head. "My head feels quite light now," she joked, but her face was sad as she looked down at the shiny locks scattered around her feet.

"You'll need something on your head," her mother said, pulling out a turban from a box and handing it to her daughter who placed it carefully on top of her cropped hair.

"How do I look?" Julianna asked.

"You look like a beautiful boy," her mother replied in a shaky voice, pulling her daughter into her arms and hugging her tightly. "You're a good girl, Julianna. I pray the gods will bless you and keep you safe."

Chapter two

The following morning Julianna got up early. The sadness over her lost hair had passed, and now she was filled with excitement as she thought of the adventure ahead.

"I need to go out early," she had told her mother, "before Father wakes up, or he may forbid me to go. You must call me Jules from now on," she said as she dressed in her boy's clothes. "It's important that no one realises I'm a girl."

Quietly they carried out twenty bundles of the spun yarn from the workshop to the yard outside and loaded them onto their donkey. "That should be enough for today," Lilah said when the bags hanging from the donkey were full.

"What will you say if anyone sees me and wonders who I am?" Julianna asked her mother, stroking the donkey's ears as she spoke.

"Well," Lilah replied, "I shall tell Lois and Dorcas not to say anything; they know how to keep a secret. And to anyone else I shall say you are my nephew and you have come to help out while Timon is ill."

Julianna grasped the rope around the donkey's neck. "Goodbye, Mum," she said, kissing her mother, "I'll see you this afternoon. Wish me luck."

"Goodbye, my love," Lilah replied, "Do take care."

She stood, watching as her daughter set off with a wave towards the market. Once Lilah had been a beauty and she still had the fine features and slim figure of her youth. But time and anxiety had drawn worry lines around her eyes and she had a habit of biting her bottom lip when she was worried, which she was doing again now.

At last when her daughter was out of sight, Lilah turned back into the house and quickly knelt down beside the household shrine which held several statues of Greek gods. Lilah didn't have much faith in them, although she liked to pray to Hestia, the goddess of the home, who she thought might understand best how worried she was.

After a few minutes, Julianna found herself walking alongside a vineyard and she noticed that the grapes were ready for picking. Tying the donkey to the fence post she looked around her, and seeing no one, she quickly ducked under the fence and gathered a handful of beautiful red grapes. They won't miss a few, she thought as she continued on her way eating the sweet juicy fruit. They were good. It seemed a long time since she had eaten anything other than dry bread and the occasional orange from the tree in their garden.

The path led up a hill before going down again to the market place and the city centre. She paused at the brow of the hill to take in the view. In one direction she had a clear view of the great temple of the goddess Artemis, or Diana, as the Romans called her. Its impressive marble sculptured columns and huge statue of the goddess dominated the landscape.

She turned in the other direction and took in the view of the city of Ephesus. It was a stunning sight. It lay in a valley between two hills with the valley sloping towards the sea. Ephesus had two public squares. The nearest one was the civic square where city business was done. This was dedicated to the goddess Hestia and had a sacred flame burning that was never allowed to go out.

Beyond the civic square was the commercial square holding most of the market stalls. This was where she was heading. She could faintly see people like ants moving round setting up their stalls. Behind the market was the temple of Octavia and to the right another temple to Apollo. Beyond that she could see, built into the hillside, the Great Theatre where thousands of people could sit and see gladiators fighting, watch plays or listen to concerts. And away in the distance was the sea with the port where ships from all around the Mediterranean came, carrying olive oil, marble, wine, and grain as well as slaves to those waiting to buy them.

Looking at the great city ahead, Julianna suddenly felt very afraid. This was madness! How was she going to cope in the market alone? And could she convince people she was a boy?

Chapter three

"Hey, dreamer!" a laughing voice called, "are you standing there all day? Only you're blocking the path!"

Julianna jumped, and turned to see a boy a few years older than her, standing on the path behind, with two donkeys laden down with huge rolls of cloth. She flushed red and with a mumbled "Sorry" hastily moved on down the track towards the market place.

As she made her way she was conscious of the boy following behind. She was suddenly more aware of how she must look, and grasped more tightly to the donkey's rope. As a girl she wore her skirts at a modest length down to the ankles. But now that she was a boy she was wearing a much shorter tunic and she could feel the wind against her bare legs. Would he realise she was a girl? She felt very vulnerable and scared.

"What's your name, boy?" The older boy had caught up with her now and was looking down at her with a grin. He was a head taller than her and had spiky black hair under a bright blue turban.

She breathed a sigh of relief. "Jules," she replied and the name sounded strange in her ears. "What's yours?"

"My name's Zakaria, but my friends call me Zak," he replied. He had a friendly open face with honest eyes. "I've not seen you before. Have you just moved into this area?"

The girl hesitated, "Yes, I've recently come to help my uncle who's not well," she lied.

"Where have you come from?" Zak continued.

"Oh," Julianna caught her breath. She hadn't been prepared for all these questions. "I come from the other side of Ephesus," she said waving vaguely in the direction of the port.

They were now quite close to the market and Julianna saw with a sigh of relief the spot where her father set up stall. "I'm going this way," she said, turning off the path as she spoke.

"Well, I'm going on a bit further," Zak said. "It's good to meet you, Jules," he continued. "I hope we bump into each other again. Us lads need to stick together."

"Bye, Zak," she replied, more cheerful now. "See you again."

Julianna had no time to think about the boy as she quickly tied up the donkey and began to unload the bundles of yarn and display them carefully on the ground. She remembered how her father had piled them up in pyramids so that they could be seen from a distance. She put the thin woollen yarn that people might buy to weave cloth into one pyramid and the thicker thread which was mostly used for sewing in another and then stood back to admire her work.

"Well, hallo, son," came a man's friendly voice from the stall next door, as he emerged from behind a stack of tent posts. "You must belong to Timon. I can see the family likeness. How is he? We've not seen him here for some time."

Julianna turned to see the man who was speaking to her. She recognised him as one of her father's friends, but tried not to show that she knew him. "Hallo, Sir," she said. "Yes, I'm his nephew. Jules is my name. Uncle Timon isn't at all well so I've come over to help him out." She felt quite proud of herself remembering to call him Uncle.

"I'm sorry to hear that," the man replied. "It's good he has you. By the look of it you've got quite a lot of thread there to sell. I hope you do well today son."

The market was beginning to get busy now and the man turned from talking to her to shout out, "Tents and tent posts for sale! Good prices!" A few stalls away she heard another man shouting, "Buy your household gods here! Beautiful silver models of Artemis and the temple!"

Julianna gulped. She had forgotten she would have to shout out too. 'I hope my voice isn't too girlish,' she thought. She took a breath and called out, "Good quality yarn," but her voice was lost in the noise and clamour of people pushing through the market and the occasional donkey braying. Her voice would have to be louder if she was going to sell anything. "Sewing thread for sale!" she shouted at the top of her voice and one or two turned to look at her stall.

"Let's have a look at your sewing thread, lad," a customer demanded. After examining it carefully he said, "Fine, I'll have four bundles," and put one denarius into Julianna's outstretched hand. Her heart swelled with pride as she put the money into the leather bag around her waist. Today they would eat a proper meal.

Chapter four

By the afternoon Julianna had sold seven bundles of wool and six bundles of sewing thread. The market stalls were beginning to pack up as people made their way home to avoid the heat of the afternoon sun. Quickly she stacked the seven remaining bundles onto the donkey. She was keen to get to the bread and fish stall before going home.

"Goodbye!" she called to the man in the next stall. "See you tomorrow."

"Bye, lad," the man replied. "Tell your Uncle Timon that Lucas asked after him and wishes him well."

"I will," she replied.

The bread stall had just a few rolls left so she bought six and then went quickly to the fish stall where she bought two large fish. She saw some fresh figs on the fruit stall and bought a small bag of those too. Then she turned the donkey towards the path that led to her part of town.

A great weariness came over her as she made her way up. She stopped by a well and gave herself and her donkey a drink. Seeing a patch of shade under an olive tree nearby, she decided to sit down for a while.

"How did you get on, Jules?" a voice called and she looked up to see Zak beside the well getting himself and his donkeys a drink too.

Julianna smiled, "Oh, hallo, Zak," she replied. Having been a boy all day she was now much more confident. "I did quite well, thanks, sold enough to provide a meal for us all and pay the workers, so I'm pleased. How about you?"

Zak frowned, "Not too good today," he said dropping down beside her. "People aren't buying woven cloth for tents so much. More of them want leather or linen. I've told my grandfather we need to move with the times but he's kept goats and used their hair for cloth all his life and finds it hard to change."

"Grandfather?" she enquired trying to ignore the fact that she could feel Zak's arm against hers as they sat together under the tree. She felt very uncomfortable. He wouldn't be sitting so close to me if he knew I was a girl she thought. "Don't you have a father?" she went on.

"Oh yes, I have a father," Zak said bitterly, "but he's too interested in making money and mixing with his women friends to bother about me." He paused for a while, staring angrily down at the ground.

"I'm sorry," Julianna said.

"And my mother is dead," Zak went on, answering her question before she asked it. "I live with my mother's parents. They're very good to me." He looked up, "What about you?"

Julianna paused. What could she tell her new friend? "I live with my mother and father," she said, "five miles or so away. They also have a spinning business."

"They must miss you now that you're with your Uncle," Zak said.

"Yes," she replied, "but my father is very strong and has several people working for him. Not like Uncle Timon. When he's well I'll be going back home."

"Well then, I hope he doesn't get well too soon!" Zak said laughing, but Julianna didn't smile back.

She jumped to her feet. "I must be going," she said quickly. "They'll be wondering where I am."

"Me too," Zak said, and the two of them took hold of their donkeys' ropes and began the walk up the hill. "I won't see you tomorrow" he said as they walked.

"Why's that?" Julianna asked.

"It's Saturday, the Jewish Sabbath. We don't work on the Sabbath," Zak said.

"Why ever not?" Julianna asked in surprise.

"We believe God made the world in six days and after that he rested. He has told us that we should also rest and worship Him on the seventh day," Zak answered.

"Which god is that?" she asked. "I rather like a god who tells you to have a rest!"

"Oh, I forgot, you're not Jewish, are you?" Zak said. "We only have one God. We call him Yahweh."

"That's weird," Julianna replied. "Greeks believe there are lots of gods, one for the trees, one for the sea, one for the rivers, one for the hills," she waved her arms around as she spoke, "and loads of others."

"Not all Greeks believe that," Zak said, "I know a few who believe in the Jewish Messiah the same as us."

Julianna shook her head, "I have no idea what you're talking about," she said, "and this is where I turn off to my home, so you'll have to tell me more another day."

"I will," Zak said, "Bye, Jules. Maybe see you in a day or so."

"Bye Zak," she replied, turning to run up the last few yards to her home.

Chapter five

"Oh thank the gods you are home, Julianna!" Lilah jumped up from her seat beside Timon as she saw her daughter's smiling face at the door. "How did you get on? You're looking very pleased with yourself."

"I did well, Mother," Julianna answered holding out the money in one hand and the food in the other. "Tonight we can eat a good meal and tomorrow we can pay the women."

"Oh, well done!" her mother cried, clapping her hands with happiness. Quickly she took the fish from her daughter. "That's wonderful," she sighed, and pulled out a board and a knife to begin preparing it.

"Lucas wishes you well," Julianna said, sitting down next to her father as she spoke and taking his hand in hers. "How do you feel today?" she asked anxiously looking at his pale face.

Timon smiled at his daughter. "I'm fine," he said, "I've not coughed so much today. In a few days I'll be up and about, you'll see. But tell me, how did you get on being a boy today?"

Julianna laughed. "Fine," she said, "I met another boy who sells cloth for tents. He works for his Grandfather. And he says he's a Jew and someone called a Messiah is coming soon. I had no idea what he was talking about." She chatted on happily, telling her father all about her day as the room began to fill with the delicious smell of frying fish. "Tomorrow I shall go again and sell more thread. You won't mind if I go, will you, Father?" she asked, looking down at him. But his eyes were closed and he was asleep.

"Well," Lilah said, "you seem to have sent him off to sleep with all your chatter! Never mind, you come and eat your fish and your father can have his when he wakes. You must be starving."

Indeed she did feel very hungry, and the taste of the fish and bread rolls was even more sweet because she had earned the money for them herself.

As she ate Lilah questioned her, "What is the name of the boy you met today?" she asked her daughter anxiously. "Is he a good boy? I wouldn't want him to lead you into trouble."

"His name's Zak," Julianna replied. "I think he's good, but I suppose I'll find out if he isn't. He says he's a Jew. What's the difference between Jews and Greeks, Mother? And what is a Messiah?"

Lilah paused to think. "Well, Jews originally came from the area round Jerusalem but they seem to have settled all over the world. They're different from us as they don't believe in all our gods," she said.

"So what do they believe?" Julianna asked, cleaning her plate with her last piece of bread. She wiped her mouth and sat back with a satisfied sigh.

"I'm not really sure," Lilah replied. "I remember your father had a friend who was a Jew who said there was only one God, the god of the Jews. As for this Messiah person, I'm not really sure, although I do remember something about a man called Apollos who visited the synagogue here. Perhaps he is the Messiah they seem to be waiting for."

"But ..." Julianna began.

"No more talk now Julianna," Lilah said with a smile. "I must wake your father and give him his supper. This fish will help build up his strength."

Julianna sank back with a sigh into the soft matting in the corner of the room and watched as her mother woke her father and gently coaxed him to eat a piece of fish and bread. It had been a very busy and eventful day. She had never been out alone before and she had enjoyed the adventure.

Timon didn't seem very hungry. He ate a few mouthfuls and then said, "That's enough thank you my dear. It was lovely." Then he lay down again and closed his eyes. He looked so pale and thin. Lilah looked across at her daughter and saw her worried face and smiled bravely. "That will do him good," she said. "Tomorrow he will eat even more and he will soon get his strength back."

Julianna nodded. How she hoped her mother was right. She wished, as she had wished so many times before, that she had been born a boy. How much easier life would be for them. Still, she thought, now that I can buy good food every day, Father will soon be well. And with a huge yawn she settled down on her mat, and fell into a deep sleep.

Chapter six

Life for Julianna fell into a regular pattern. Each day she would get up, load thread onto the donkey and make her way to the market. Often she would pause to pick grapes from the vineyard on her way, although she was careful not to if Zak was there. He might not approve. Once at the market she would set up her stall next to Lucas and work until mid afternoon.

Lucas was always concerned to hear how Timon was and when they were not busy he would tell her stories about other stall holders in the market. "That man over there," he said one day, pointing to a smart stall where the table was loaded with statues of the goddess Artemis and other silver souvenirs, "he's a silversmith. That's the best business to be in around here. Everyone wants a silver statue of the goddess in their home."

Julianna often watched enviously as many people came to his stall and the pile of silver statues got lower and lower. Life would be easy if she could sell half as much, she thought.

Occasionally she sold several bundles of wool and cord and was able to buy olives and dates and nuts as well as fish and bread but more often she was not so successful. Most days she was only able to buy red beans and bread for their supper. "There are not many shoppers at the local market," she told her mother once. "I really need to travel further to a larger market."

Lilah agreed. "Your father used to travel to Athens and to Corinth once or twice a year. He has a wealthy cousin who likes to buy our best thread. But I couldn't let you travel out of Ephesus on your own. It wouldn't be safe."

Julianna sighed and wished once more that she had been born a boy. It wasn't fair that girls had to stay at home while boys were allowed to do more exciting things.

Most days she saw Zak, although he never came down to her part of the market as his father had a stall there and he wanted to avoid seeing him. As time went on Julianna found out more about his life with his grandparents and his plans for the future. He was hoping that he would be able to learn how to work in leather. "If I can persuade Grandfather to let me," he explained.

She also found out more about his God and the mysterious Messiah. It seemed that the man Apollos that her mother had been talking about wasn't the Messiah, and anyway he wasn't in Ephesus any more, he'd gone off to preach somewhere else. Apollos was a disciple of a man called John the Baptist and he had been teaching the Jews in Ephesus that they should repent of the bad things they'd been doing and follow a man called Jesus. Jesus was apparently the Messiah who the Jewish prophets hundreds of years before had said would come and save them.

Zak and his Grandparents were very excited about this man Jesus. They had never met him as he hadn't travelled as far as Ephesus, but the rumours were that he had gone around doing amazing miracles and teaching about a new kingdom where he would be King.

"What kind of miracles?" Julianna asked Zak when they were sitting by the well gulping down mouthfuls of water after a busy day at the market.

"Well," Zak replied, pulling off his turban and running his fingers through his thick dark hair, "I don't know a lot about it, but our leaders, Aquila and Priscilla, told us that he had made blind people see, deaf people hear, and people who hadn't been able to move for years he made them get up and walk. They say he even ..." and here Zak paused, and his voice dropped to a whisper, "he even brought dead people back to life again."

Julianna paused taking in this news, "I wish he was here now," she said sadly, "maybe he could heal my fa..." she stopped and gave a quick cough, "... maybe he could heal my uncle."

Zak gave her a sharp look and for a moment she thought he was going to say something, but just then they were interrupted by the sound of shouting. Curiously they watched a group of men in the distance moving down the path towards them. They seemed to be arguing about something and two of them seemed very angry. Suddenly Zak jumped to his feet and dragged Julianna into the shadow of an olive tree. "It's him!" he hissed as the noisy group drew closer.

"Who?" Julianna whispered back trying in vain to see the men over Zak's shoulder. Zak didn't answer but just stood there holding her arm tightly as the men passed. She was puzzled. It wasn't like Zak to be afraid.

"That was my father," Zak explained when the men were out of sight, "I don't want to get involved in his fights. I expect he's cheated someone out of money. They're wasting their time if they think they'll get anything out of him." He spat on the ground in disgust. "Come on, Jules, let's go home."

Chapter seven

They were silent for a while as they climbed the hill together. But by the time they reached the top where the path separated Zak was his cheerful self again. For a moment they stood looking down at the city in the valley below and, away in the distance, the brilliant blue sea dotted with tiny ships.

"Ephesus—the light of Asia!" Zak suddenly said. "The writer Pliny was right. Do you remember learning about him at school, Jules?"

Julianna's heart missed a beat. "Oh, yes," she said vaguely, "he was right, Ephesus is a beautiful city." She hoped he wouldn't ask her any more as she'd never been to school and hadn't heard of the writer!

Fortunately, Zak was already thinking of something else. "I'm probably going to Athens next week," he told her. "We have a large order from a market owner in Athens who has offered us a good price for our cloth. And during the games season we try to make a trip to Corinth as they're getting ready for hundreds of travellers who'll be coming to the Isthmian games. In the next few months Corinth will become a city of tents."

"How long does it take to get there?" Julianna asked.

"Two days by boat to Athens, and then a day's journey to Corinth. Why don't you come with me, Jules? It's a good place to do business. You'd sell loads of cord; all the tent makers and repairers will be needing it."

"I'd like to," Julianna replied. "My uncle has a relation in Athens who buys thread from us. He used to go over quite often, but they're not happy about me travelling so far."

"That's a shame," Zak said. "It would have been fun to have some company. Anyway, time I was off. See you tomorrow, Jules."

Julianna turned slowly towards home. Could she persuade her mother to let her go with Zak, she wondered? It was doubtful. She was lost in thought so she didn't notice two older boys sitting nearby watching her. It wasn't until they jumped onto the path in front of her that she realised that they were up to no good.

"Hey, little boy," the bigger one said pointing to her leather bag, "what have you got there?"

Bravely she faced them, clutching the bag of money more tightly. "Please get out of my way," she said as firmly as she could, trying not to show how frightened she was.

The other boy came up close to her and looked into her face. "What a pretty boy you are!" he said, reaching out towards her. "Now I'm sure you'd be very happy to let us look inside your leather bag."

"No!" she cried, and then everything seemed to happen at once. Julianna shouted for help and the donkey let out a loud cry as one of the boys made a grab at the bag. But she was holding on to it so tightly that she was pulled to the ground still holding onto her precious earnings. One boy twisted her arm while the other pulled at the bag until she was forced to let go. In the struggle the bag broke open and the money she had earned that day spilled out around them.

From her place on the ground Julianna watched helplessly as the two youths began gathering up the coins. In the distance she could see her mother at the door of their little house waiting, as she often did, for her daughter to return. Lilah could see the girl was in trouble and with a shout began to run towards them. But she was too far away. The two boys had already collected up the coins and were turning to run in the opposite direction. Julianna tried to get up, but a twinge in her ankle forced her back down and she saw that her leg was bleeding. The pain made her eyes fill with tears and she angrily brushed them away.

Then suddenly she heard another shout, followed by cries of pain. Quickly she looked back and saw, to her amazement, the two boys cowering on the ground. Standing over them with a large roll of cloth in his hand was a grim faced Zak. "You'd better hand over that money," she heard him say, "or I'll hit you both again."

By this time her mother had reached Julianna and had helped her up. "Julianna, are you alright?" she asked anxiously. "Yes," the girl said quickly, "and I'm Jules, your nephew," she hissed. Lilah widened her eyes and nodded, her hand covering her mouth. "Don't worry," Jules said with a tearful laugh, "there's too much noise up there for anyone to have heard you."

Together they watched the scene open-mouthed as the two youths scrambled to their feet, rubbing the back of their legs which showed red marks where the roll had hit them and staggered away. The money was left behind on the ground.

Zak picked up the money and came towards them putting it into Lilah's outstretched hand.

"What can I say?" she said gripping his arm, "I am so grateful to you."

Zak looked pleased but embarrassed. "I saw those two earlier and wondered if they were going to cause trouble," he explained, "so when I heard Jules shout I came back. These cloth rolls make a good weapon," he added laughing.

"They certainly do," Lilah said admiringly, "and you were very brave to come to our help. You must be Zak. I've heard all about you."

Zak looked at Julianna. "Jules, your ankle is swelling up, and you're bleeding," he observed. "Let's get you home." And before they could protest he picked her up and carried her along the path and into the house.

Chapter eight

After that, it was easier to persuade her mother to let her go to Athens.

Lilah had been very impressed by the care Zak showed as he carried her daughter into the house and placed her gently on a bench inside the door. Then while she examined Julianna's ankle and washed the cuts on her legs he had gone over to Timon and sat with him.

Julianna watched him shyly. He had lifted her up so easily and it felt wonderful to be in his arms. With Zak around she would always feel safe, she thought. But whatever would he think if he knew she was a girl?

"There we are, Jules," her mother said finally as she tied the bandage around her ankle. "You should be good as new tomorrow."

Then they offered Zak some milk to drink and gave him a large skein of yarn to take home. "Here, young man," Lilah said, handing it to him, "string is always useful."

"Oh yes," Zak said gratefully, "we can use it to tie up the rolls of cloth. It's so much stronger than strips of leather."

After he had gone Julianna asked her parents about the trip to Athens. "Please let me go," she pleaded. "I know it's a long journey, but I'll be fine. Think of all the cord and yarn I could sell."

Lilah looked down at her hands, absentmindedly examining the hard skin on her palms made by the many hours of twisting the spindle. She often did this when she wasn't sure what to say. "Well," she said, half to herself, "our cousin Spiro was asking when we'd be coming his way. And Zak is a good lad," she paused looking up at Timon.

"Oh please, Father," Julianna cried, "Zak has taken the boat trip lots of times so I won't get lost."

Lilah nodded, "He would certainly make sure she was safe; he treats her like a younger brother! What do you say, Timon?"

"I'm not happy about it, but what can I do?" Timon replied slowly, despair in his voice. "I'm just lying here all day and am no use to anyone."

"Don't say that, Father," Julianna cried, running over to him. "You'll soon be better, you must get better!" And she flung herself beside her father and pressed the hand he held out to her against her hot cheek.

Timon smiled wearily. "Yes, yes, my dear," he said, then shut his eyes to hide the pain in them.

Lilah looked anxiously at her husband. He looked so ill, his face more thin and pale than she had ever seen it. "Try to drink, dear," she urged putting a cup of fresh goat's milk to his lips as she spoke. After a few sips he sank back onto the pillows as another coughing spell shook his body. The effort of talking had taken all the strength from him.

"Zak was telling me about the Messiah today, Mother," Julianna said a bit later. "His name is Jesus and Zak says he can heal any kind of illness. I'm going to find him and ask him to come to Ephesus and make Father well."

"That would be wonderful, dear, but how will you find him?" Lilah asked. "And if he's the Jewish Messiah, I'm not sure he'd be interested in an ordinary Greek. The Jews are very proud and tend to stick to their own kind."

"But Zak's not like that!" Julianna protested. "And I'm going to find Jesus and try to persuade him."

"Well, I'm sure you will," Lilah smiled sadly, patting her daughter on the head and turning into the workshop with tears in her eyes.

Dorcas and Lois looked up as she came in. "He's not so good today, is he?" Dorcas observed softly.

"But," Lois said, "with the good food that girl of yours is bringing him, he should get his strength back soon."

"I do hope so," Lilah said, but her voice sounded strained. Bravely she straightened her back and said in a stronger voice, "Can you concentrate on spinning the fine thread for the next few days please, ladies. The cousin we deal with in Athens would like to buy our best quality yarn."

Having set the women to work, Lilah turned back to her daughter. "Come, Julianna," she said softly, "we need to plan your trip."

Chapter nine

It was a week later that Jules and Zak set off. Julianna had already said her goodbyes to her parents as they had agreed that they mustn't be too affectionate when she left, in case Zak or his Grandfather became suspicious. "I'm only your nephew, after all," Julianna said as she hugged them.

Zak's Grandfather had come to pick her up with his donkey cart. He wasn't as old as she had expected and had a cheerful face with red cheeks and sparkling grey eyes. When they were introduced she immediately felt comfortable with him. He helped to put the bundles of fine thread into the back along with the rolls of cloth, and then spent a little while talking to Lilah. "I'll call in to see you and your husband while Jules is away," he promised. "You must let us know if there is anything we can do to help."

Then he turned and climbed onto the cart. "Up you get you two," he called, "we need to get going or you'll miss the boat. It won't wait," he told them, "once it has been loaded with the cargo it's taking to Athens, it will be off."

Jules looked back as they set off along the rough track and gave a last wave. "See you in a week!" she called cheerfully. "Bye, Auntie!"

Even though it was early morning already, the heat from sun was strong. "It's going to be hot today,"

Grandfather said. "You lads make sure you keep out of the sun on deck. You won't realise you are burning with the sea breeze."

"Yes, Grandfather," Zak said meekly.

"And Zak, you make sure you look after young Jules. His aunt is relying on you."

"Yes, Grandfather," Zak said again with a wink at Jules.

His Grandfather looked across at him and chuckled. "Don't Grandfather me!" he said. "Just remember your responsibilities!"

The great seaport of Ephesus was coming closer. Jules had never been down to the port before, although she had a view of the sea every day, and she was trembling with excitement as they drew nearer to the docks. She remembered her father telling her about the great wealth of Ephesus. "You should be proud to be born in such an important city," he had told her. "It is the second largest city in the Roman empire—Rome is the largest of course."

Jules watched engrossed as traders in donkey carts and horse drawn wagons moved towards the docks loaded down with containers of olive oil, bags of grain, pottery vessels and animals to load onto the waiting ships.

"We must be near to your home," Zak said to her. "It's a shame we can't call in on your parents to say hallo before we set sail, but we don't have time."

Jules stared at him confused for a moment. "Oh, yes," she stammered. "They live a few miles in that direction," she said waving vaguely in the direction to their right. She breathed a sigh of relief. Thank goodness they didn't have time.

"That was very thoughtless of me," Zak's Grandfather said. "I should have allowed an extra hour. Never mind, maybe on the way back we can visit."

"Yes, maybe," Jules said with a sinking feeling. She would have to make some kind of excuse, but for now she was safe. This was the trouble with one lie; it seemed to lead to others and could get very complicated.

They were drawing into the docks now and Jules could see a dozen or so ships moored up, their sails hanging limply from the masts. The sounds of men shouting as they ran to and fro, and of animals protesting as they were pushed into small enclosures on the ships grew louder and louder as they pulled up close to the ships.

They watched in silence as packages of all shapes and sizes were quickly lifted onto the deck and stowed by sailors into the hold below. Only a few of the smaller traders like Zak and Jules were getting onto the ships with their cargo as most of the larger traders had dealers in Athens who would collect the goods at their end.

"This ship is ours," Zak told Jules, pointing to the one nearest them, "the one with blue sails there."

Jules looked where he was pointing. There was a large group of women and a few men standing silently beside the ship and as they grew closer Jules could see they were chained to each other. Some were about her age.

"Slaves," Grandfather said in answer to her unspoken question. His voice was sad. "Ephesus is the slave capital of the world," he went on, "and almost everyone in Athens has a slave. That's where a lot of our wealth in Ephesus comes from."

They were alongside the ship now and as Grandfather secured the donkey Jules watched slaves being herded onto the ship and packed into a container like animals. The sailors were already beginning to untie the mooring ropes and preparing to set sail. "Hurry now," Grandfather said as they unloaded the cart, "you get up onto the deck Zak and I'll throw the stuff up to you. Jules, you get your bags and follow."

The next few minutes were a scramble of activity and at last all was stowed in the hold and Zak and Jules were standing on the bow waving goodbye to his Grandfather.

"Take care, both of you," he called to them. "And remember what I told you, Zak!"

"Yes, Grandfather," Zak said laughing, "see you soon."

Then the two friends watched as the sailors skilfully pulled on the sheet until the sails caught the wind and the ship moved into the open water of the Aegean Sea.

Chapter ten

"Let's find a good place to settle, Jules," Zak said when the port of Ephesus was just a dot on the landscape. "We'll have to live and sleep on deck but it's only for two nights and as long as we keep out of the way of the sailors we'll be fine."

"And out of the sun," Jules reminded him, stretching out her now suntanned legs as they sat down behind a large container of wheat. She was still thinking about the slaves in a container on the other side of the ship. "Poor things," she said, "what will happen to them now?"

"It's sad," Zak agreed. "They'll end up being sold at the slave market in Athens and some will have quite a good life if they have kind masters, but others ..." his voice trailed off.

"For others, it will be worse than death," Jules said finishing Zak's sentence. "I feel so sorry for the young girls," she continued. "They'll never be able to marry or have a normal life."

"What sort of girl do you want to marry, Jules?" Zak asked.

"What?" she asked in confusion, her face burning red at his question.

"'Well," Zak went on laughing, "in a couple of years I'll be seventeen and will have to choose a wife. You're only thirteen, so you're still young, although if you were a girl you'd be married off in a year or so."

Jules felt her anger rising. "Married off indeed" she thought, just like selling off a cow. It took all her self-control not to tell him she was one of those girls he was talking about.

"Obviously the girl I marry will have to be beautiful," Zak said, oblivious of her clenched fist and red face. "She'd need to be clever too so that I could have a conversation with her. I want her to be a good cook and able to make my life comfortable. And I wouldn't want a giggly girl who only talks about clothes or babies. What about you, Jules?"

Jules tried to swallow her annoyance. "What she looks like isn't important," she said crossly. "I'd like a wife who will go travelling with me and who would help in the business. I don't want one to just stay at home and cook. Anyway," she finished, "I'm not going to get married for years."

They were quiet for a while and looked out to sea both lost in their own thoughts. The sky was blue and the sea a deep turquoise. The only sounds at that moment were the flapping of the sails, the soft swishing of the sea against the side of the ship and the cry of the seagulls overhead.

It was time to change the subject. "What's Athens like?" Jules asked, "Is it as big as Ephesus? Are the people the same as us?"

Zak turned to look at her. "Athens used to be a flourishing city even bigger than Ephesus but these days it's much smaller—maybe twenty-five times smaller!" he said. "It's still the university centre of the world though. It's where the great philosophers like Socrates, Plato and

Aristotle taught. You'll remember learning about them at school."

"Oh yes," Jules replied and hoped he wouldn't ask for her opinion on these great men's teaching as, being a girl, she'd never been to school. "Well," she said quickly, "if it's a smaller city, it shouldn't be too hard to find my Uncle's cousin."

After a while the two sat down and opened the packages of food that Julianna's mother and Zak's Grandmother had made up for them to sustain them on their journey. "There's enough food here for a month," Jules gasped looking at Zak as he filled his mouth with cheese and bread and olives. "Although," she added, "not if you eat like that all the time."

The food was good and the sea air had made them both hungry. When they had finished they sat back with a sigh and for a while dozed off in the shade of the wheat container as the ship danced through the waters.

Zak was the first to wake and sat quietly watching his friend doze. She opened her eyes to find him looking at her in a considering kind of way which made her feel uncomfortable. She said the first thing that came into her head, "Zak, tell me where will I find Jesus."

"You won't!" Zak said in surprise.

"That's what my aunt said," Jules replied, "but I'm determined to find him and ask him to heal my uncle."

"But you won't find him," Zak said again. "He's dead. Well, not exactly, he was dead but he's in heaven now."

Jules felt her world crashing around her. "But you said he was the Messiah and was going to be a King!" she exclaimed. "What kind of miracle worker gets himself killed? And what use is he to anyone in heaven, wherever that is!" She turned away from Zak in disgust, her eyes full of tears.

"I'm sorry, Jules," Zak said, "it's a bit of a long story, and I'm not sure I've got it all straight in my head yet. I know more about John the Baptist than Jesus, and John had his head chopped off. Aquila and Priscilla would be able to explain it better. The thing is that Jesus was crucified by the Romans a few years back. But after three days he came back to life again and was seen by hundreds of people, so it wasn't a made up story. Then it seems he said goodbye to his followers, told them to continue his work and then disappeared into heaven. He was never seen again."

"So," Jules said bitterly, "why do you still follow him, or John the Baptist for that matter? If they didn't have the power to save themselves then how can they save anyone else? What a weird god you have, Zak. I don't want to hear any more about him. At least our gods are around us here and not up in heaven." And with that she folded her arms and shut her eyes again pretending to be asleep.

So, Jesus was in heaven and she would never be able to ask him to heal her father.

Chapter eleven

For the next couple of hours the two friends didn't talk much. Zak realised his friend was upset so wisely kept quiet. He left her for a while and went to speak to some of the sailors who were off duty sitting on the deck drinking watered-down wine. She sat watching him and wishing she had the confidence to just wander up to them and chat. I might look like a boy on the outside, she thought, but inside I'm still a girl. Zak must think I'm a very silly boy.

Bravely Jules sat up straight and forced herself to think of her adventure ahead so that by the time Zak returned to join her she had pulled herself together.

"It seems we're in for a bit of a storm," Zak said, dropping down beside her. "The sailors seem to think those black clouds ahead will hit us in the next hour or so. We'll need to go down into the hold to keep dry."

They waited for a while and watched as the wind grew stronger and the threatening clouds grew closer. By now the sailors had gone back to their posts and were preparing for the storm ahead.

"Come on, time to get going," Zak said, pulling Jules to her feet and steadying her as the ship lurched to one side. Together they staggered towards the entrance to the hold and almost fell down the wooden steps and onto a sack of grain.

It took a moment for the two to become accustomed to the dark. They stood looking at all the containers of olive oil and sacks of grain until Jules said at last, “Look, our cargo is over there.” Zak looked at where she was pointing and saw the packages she had recognised as those containing her yarn. “Let’s sit on those,” she went on, “at least we know what’s in those bags.”

“Good idea,” Zak agreed and together they stepped over the packs of wheat until they reached the corner where they had stored their cargo. “Phew, it smells down here,” he went on. “I bet there are loads of rats and spiders around.”

Jules was glad he couldn’t see her shudder at the thought of rats running over their feet or spiders crawling over her face. What made it worse was the thought of the sea creatures and mermaids who became fierce and cruel during a storm. She didn’t mention those to Zak as she knew he didn’t believe in them. “Well, at least it’s dry,” she said bravely. “Listen to that rain now!”

The rain was hammering loudly onto the deck and the sailors could be heard running to and fro as the captain shouted orders. The wind had really got up and was tossing the solid ship around as if it was made of paper. Fortunately, the hold was well stacked and there wasn’t too much room for the cargo to move around. The two friends sat in the dark being rocked from side to side for what seemed to be an age, listening to the storm outside.

It seemed to go on forever, but at last the wind and rain eased off and they were able to make themselves more comfortable. "It's time we had our supper," Zak remarked. "I think we should eat and then settle down here for the night. It will be too wet to sleep on deck."

Reluctantly Jules agreed. She shivered, "It's cold too. The rain has cooled the air and now that it's getting dark it'll be even colder on the deck."

It took them a while to see where the bag of food was but eventually they found it under some containers of olive oil where it had fallen during the storm. Jules didn't feel very hungry after being thrown around but it hadn't affected Zak who greedily tucked into his bread and fish as if nothing had happened. She ate a few dates and a small piece of bread, being careful not to drop any onto the floor for fear of attracting a mouse or rat.

After that they settled down to sleep. "We should sleep close together," Zak said, "to keep each other warm." He lay down next to her and she felt her heart pounding at his closeness. Thank goodness it was dark. She could feel his breath on her hot cheek and his arm against hers. "Good night, Jules," Zak said. "Sleep well." And within a few minutes he was fast asleep.

It took Julianna a lot longer to settle. She had never been so close to a boy, and she knew that it was forbidden to sleep next to one like this unless you were married. But what could she do? It was important that he believed her to be a boy or it would be the end of her adventures with him. If he found out, she would have to swear him to secrecy. But even then their friendship would end, and she was beginning to realise how important Zak was becoming in her life.

In the end she fell asleep too, and it wasn't until they heard the sounds of sailors on the deck above shouting for their breakfast that they awoke.

Chapter twelve

"There's Athens," Zak said. "Can you see it in the distance?"

It was the end of the second day on the ship. After the storm the sea had changed its mood so they had gone back on the deck and stood watching the ship cutting its way through the now calm waters.

The captain had informed them that they should be ready to disembark first, and already they had hauled up their bags and were waiting for the port to come into view.

"Yes, I see it," Jules said. Her eyes took in the bright white houses on the hillside, and trees with brilliant pink flowers set against the deepest blue sky. "It looks beautiful," she said, "and I'll be very glad to get off this ship."

"Me too," Zak agreed, "Two days is a long time when there's nothing to do." He paused. "But once we land we'll be busy. First we'll have to get all our bags off. I'll get off first and you can throw them down to me. Then we'll need to hire a donkey and cart. There's no way we'll be able to carry all our bags without one. Now," he instructed Jules, "the main thing is, not to look too keen. We need to keep cool as if we're not bothered whether we get a cart or not. That way we'll get a better deal."

"OK," Jules said, "I'll leave that bit to you." She felt a bit sick with excitement and apprehension. Would she be able to find her father's cousin? Would he recognise her? The last time he had visited their home must have been five years ago. She would recognise him but she hoped she had changed enough that he wouldn't know it was her. It was just important to remember to say what she had planned and all would be well. All the same, she was anxious.

They were getting close to the harbour now and the sailors were skilfully turning the sails into the wind to get the boat at the right angle. Then at the last minute two of the sailors holding the mooring ropes jumped onto the quayside and in a well practised move brought the boat alongside the quay with hardly a bump.

Zak grabbed two of the heaviest bags and was quickly down the steps onto dry land. "OK," he called up, "throw down the rest!" As fast as she could Jules tossed the bags one after another into Zak's hands and then scrambled down herself and stood beside him, her legs feeling very wobbly. As they moved their bags a little distance from the ship they found themselves surrounded by men and boys all wanting to help with their baggage.

"No thanks," Zak said, "we're fine." And he promptly sat on one of the bags and indicated that Jules should do the same. "Look bored," he instructed her. "Pretend it looks as if we're waiting for someone to come for us." She did as he said and after a while the clamouring group around them moved on to hassle other passengers.

Jules looked out towards the water's edge where there was a mass of red poppies growing up around the white rocks lining the shore. How lovely it was, she thought. If only her mother and father were here with her. How they would enjoy the trip. She turned and watched the sheep and goats being taken off the ship and led away. They were followed by the slaves, still chained together. She watched sadly as they were taken up the same path. "I suppose they're all going to market," she said to herself, "animals and slaves all together." The beauty of the place somehow made the cruelty greater.

"Come on, Jules, stop daydreaming!" she heard Zak shout and she turned to find he was already piling the bags onto a cart with the help of a thin-looking lad not much older than them. Quickly she helped with the last bags and jumped up beside Zak as the lad took the reins and began leading the cart towards the city centre.

"Where to?" the lad asked.

"The home of Spiro," Jules answered, pulling out a paper from her tunic pocket. "He lives on Philosopher's Street, near Mars Hill. He has a workshop repairing tents and furnishings. Do you know him?"

To her relief he replied, "Yup. I know him. Hold tight," and with that he set off at an alarmingly fast speed considering the load the poor donkey was carrying.

Chapter thirteen

Athens seemed quite similar to Ephesus, Jules thought, although here there seemed to be more images of gods. Almost around every corner there was a statue of some god or other, and people stopped to put flowers or fruit in front of the statue. Maybe, Jules thought, she would find a god in Athens who could heal her father.

"This is it," the thin lad finally said, drawing the cart up alongside a fine white house surrounded by shrubs and trees. Jules recognised the bay tree because of its shiny leaves but there were others with huge red and white flowers that she'd not seen before. She wanted to exclaim how lovely they were but told herself that boys weren't interested in flowers.

Over the door of the house was a large sign which said "Spiro's repair shop" in large letters and underneath in smaller letters "Expert repairers of tents and fine furnishings". There was also a symbol of a fish on the corner of the sign.

"Wait here," Zak told the cart driver. "We need to unload some of the bags and then I need you to carry me and the rest of the bags on to Apollo Street."

The lad got down from the donkey cart and sat watching as Zak began pulling off the bags containing the thread. "You go and find your cousin while I do this," he said to Jules, and rather nervously she moved towards the house.

Before she could get to the door it was opened by a short, round lady with curly grey hair. It was Spiro's wife Moria. "Hallo," she said, "is that what I hope it is? A delivery from Timon?"

"Oh yes, it is," Jules replied.

"Excellent!" the woman replied and turning back to the house called, "Spiro! Come and help. Timon has sent us thread!"

Spiro appeared behind his wife. He was as tall as his wife was short but just as plump as she was. "At last!" he exclaimed, squeezing past his wife to go down with Jules to help Zak unload. "Now we can get on with the curtain repairs for the centurion's house. I've completely run out of fine thread."

"Come in, come in," Moria said as the three returned to the door with the bags of thread. "Now where are you two lads headed for?" she continued as she noticed the donkey cart outside still laden with Zak's bags.

"I've got to deliver some of these packs to my contact in Apollo Street," Zak replied, "but Jules can stay here while I do that."

"Very good," Moria continued, "then you must come back and have a meal and spend a day or two with us here. We want to hear all the news."

Spiro was looking intently at Jules, and her heart sank. "Do I know you?" he asked. "You look a bit familiar."

Jules went hot all over. "Oh" she said quickly, "I'm Timon's nephew. I expect there's a family likeness."

"Strange, I can't remember Timon having any nephews. I know he had a daughter."

"I'm his nephew on my mother's side," Jules interrupted quickly.

Spiro scratched his head. "That's funny," he said puzzled, "I thought Lilah was an only child, didn't you Moria?"

Moria was looking at Jules. "Yes, I thought so too," she murmured. The lad had gone very red and was looking extremely uncomfortable and almost frightened, she thought.

Juels laughed but it sounded hysterical in her ears. "Oh you must have forgotten," she said, her voice rising as she spoke. "My aunt had a younger sister, she's called ..." her brain frantically tried to think of a name, "... her name's Priscilla," she blurted out. Wildly she looked at Zak who was busy packing the bags into the corner of the room. He didn't seem to be listening to the conversation. "Zak, you'd better go," she called across to him urgently. "The donkey driver will be getting impatient."

"Yes, off you go, Zak," Moria said, leading him to the door. "Come back soon and I'll have a meal ready on your return."

As soon as the donkey cart had moved off towards Apollo street, Moria turned to Jules and said, "Now sit down, lad, and tell us what's troubling you." She looked so concerned and her voice was so kind that Julianna sat down and promptly burst into tears.

Chapter fourteen

"I'm Julianna!" she cried between sobs. "Timon and Lilah's daughter. He is so very ill and there was no one else to bring the thread. But, oh please, you mustn't tell Zak! If he found out I wasn't a boy I wouldn't be allowed to travel with him."

Gradually Spiro and Moria got the whole story from the girl. They were very shocked of course, but could see the desperate situation the family were in. "Now, don't worry about anything," Spiro said at last. "Your secret is safe with us. We won't mention any more about it. While you are here you are Jules, a nephew of Timon and daughter of Priscilla—but where did that name come from?" he finished with a laugh.

"It was the name of someone who teaches in Ephesus," Jules replied. "Zak is always talking about her and her husband Aquila. They seem to be leaders of someone called Jesus who was a healer but is dead now," she finished sadly.

"We know them!" Spiro said. "They lived in Corinth before going to Ephesus. They were tent makers and we did some business with them. I'm so glad Zak has met them. Has he also met Paul? He was here in Athens and taught us so much! He left here to join his friends in Ephesus."

Jules looked at him in surprise. “I thought you were Greek like me,” she said. “Zak is a Jew and says there is only one god—not like us. This Jesus was supposed to be the Jewish Messiah, only I think that went a bit wrong.”

“Jesus isn’t just the Jewish Messiah, Jules,” Moria laughed. “He is for everyone! Jews! Greeks! Samaritans! Romans! Everyone! But enough for now. You need to put that thread into the workshop and I need to prepare lunch. Later on Spiro will take you round Athens and tell you all about it.”

Spiro and Moria were as good as their word. When Zak returned from delivering his cloth they made no mention of her family. They treated her as another boy. After their long journey the two found they were very hungry indeed and the smell of the food made their mouths water. Jules couldn’t remember when she had eaten such fine food. In the centre of the table was a large pot of stew containing delicious pieces of chicken and vegetables. It was seasoned with onions, salt, garlic and coriander. They ate this with fresh baked bread and drank watered-down wine. Then there were dishes of fruit—figs, grapes, apples and apricots fresh from their garden.

“What a feast!” Zak said happily, wiping his mouth as he ate a final fig. “Thank you so much.”

“You are very welcome,” Moria said, beaming and standing up to clear away the pots. Immediately Jules stood up to help but Moria pushed her down again with a little frown. Jules bit her lip as she remembered that boys didn’t help with chores: that was girl’s work. Thankfully, Spiro was still talking, and the moment passed.

"Moria likes nothing better than hungry mouths to feed. If you stayed here you'd get as fat as us!" Spiro said with a laugh, patting his stomach. "Which reminds me," he said turning to Zak, "I have to go to Corinth tomorrow, so why don't I take you with me? You can stay overnight and we can go together and do our business. You too, Jules. I may take some of your thread to sell too. Corinth is an interesting place." Before they could answer he was ushering them towards the door. "That's settled then. But now, lads, how about a walk round Athens? I want to show you where I met Paul."

After being confined on a ship for two days the two friends got up eagerly and allowed themselves to be led out into the sunshine towards the centre of Athens.

As they walked they listened while Spiro chatted on. "Moria says I talk too much," he explained to them and secretly they had to agree. Jules wasn't listening properly as he chatted on about life in Athens and how three years ago a man called Paul had come and changed his life.

She was distracted by all the altars to different gods at every street corner. Some of the idols were beautifully painted with smiling faces and outstretched arms. Others looked fierce and threatening. Some were made of stone, others of silver and gold shining brightly in the sun. Each had a place where people could lay their offering of flowers or fruit or other foods to please the gods and persuade them to answer their prayers.

Chapter fifteen

"Well, here we are," Spiro announced. "This is what began to change my life." They were standing under an altar with a sign on it which said "To the unknown god". "Moria and I often used to leave a sacrifice here," he continued, absentmindedly tracing the outline of a fish in the dust beneath the altar. "We were always worried that there might be a god that we didn't know about."

"So how did that change your life?" Zak asked looking puzzled. "I'm sure Paul wouldn't have worshipped here."

"Well of course not!" Spiro laughed as they continued walking, "And we don't either now, but we didn't know any better then. Paul had been in town for a while preaching in the synagogue to the Jews so we didn't hear about him until he started talking to the crowds in the market place."

They had reached the centre of town and sat for a while beside a well to have a drink. There was a temple to one side of the path and a number of people were busy decorating the doorways and statues with flowers. The air was filled with excitement as people gathered. Food was being brought and piled onto tables, and even from where they sat they caught the delicious smell of the spiced meats. A number of men were tuning up their instruments while a group of women dressed in brightly coloured clothes were practicing a dance. "They're preparing for the annual festival to the goddess Athena, the goddess of wisdom," Spiro explained in answer to Zak's questioning look. "Our city is named after her."

Spiro wandered over to say hallo to a man he knew, so the two friends were glad to sit and watch the preparations for the festival. A couple of the young dancers saw Zak and Jules, broke away from the group and came dancing over to where they sat. Julianna watched in disgust as they twirled and waved long coloured scarves in wide circles around them, flirting with their eyes. She looked at Zak who seemed to be enjoying the moment, laughing up at them as they whirled past. One of them dropped her scarf at his feet and he immediately picked it up and jumped up to return it to the girl.

Then the other girl dropped her scarf in front of Julianna. "Pick it up, Jules," Zak urged with a mischievous grin. "She likes you. It's your way of saying 'I like you too'!"

Julianna was red with embarrassment and anger. "No, I won't," she said sharply. "I don't like her—and I thought you said you didn't like giggly girls."

Zak seemed to find the whole thing hilarious. He could hardly get out his words for laughing. "Oh Jules," he said, "I've never met a boy like you before. Never mind, when you're a bit older you'll get more interested in girls."

Fortunately, just then Spiro returned. "Come on," he said, "I want to take you to Mars Hill, where the intellectuals often meet. Are you fit for a climb? I want to tell you the rest of my story up there."

They retraced their steps, but instead of going into Philosopher's Street they took a turning that led to the foot of a bare marble hill. "This is Mars Hill. Be careful on the steps," Spiro warned. "They're very smooth and can be steep in places." After that Spiro wasn't able to talk. It was easy for Jules and Zak, but because of Moria's food Spiro had a great deal more to carry and he was puffing and panting by the time they reached the top.

"Wow, what a view!" Zak exclaimed. "It's amazing!" Jules agreed, while Spiro stood holding his sides and gasping from the exertion. While he caught his breath they were able to gaze in silence and admire the sweeping view of Athens spread beneath their feet with mountains in the distance. To one side of them they could see another rocky hill with a huge temple on the top.

Spiro eventually got his breath back. "That hill is Acropolis and the temple on the top is called the Parthenon. It is dedicated to the goddess Athena," he explained.

Standing nearby there was a group of men who were waving their arms and arguing loudly together. "Athens is full of intellectuals," Spiro said in disgust. "They don't work for a living but instead just stand around discussing Stoic and Epicurean philosophy all day."

"What do they believe?" Zak asked with interest.

"I'm not too sure," Spiro replied. I know the Epicureans believe there is a God who isn't interested in us and they seem to just look for pleasure. The Stoics are a miserable lot who say that God is the world's soul, whatever that means. They think they should rise above the sorrows and joys of life and not get too emotional about things."

"They called Paul a 'babbler', but he's no fool!" Spiro went on. "He was educated in the best training schools in Judea and can argue with the best of them. They asked him to tell them more about his strange teaching and brought him here to do it."

Chapter sixteen

"And this ..." Spiro continued grandly, "... this is where my life changed!" He paused, and then said, "Paul was standing over there, where those men are. There was a pretty large crowd so I wandered over to listen. It was mind blowing! He said he could see we were all very religious and had noticed the altar to the unknown god. Then he said he was going to tell us about him. Well now, he had my interest!"

"Paul said that the God who made the world and everything in it is the Lord of heaven and earth and doesn't live in temples made by hands. The gods we'd been worshipping were just man-made. He said this God didn't need anything from us, but if we look for him we will find him because he wasn't far away." Spiro paused. "It made sense to me. I'd never thought about it like that before—for years I've been worshipping idols made in someone's workshop! But this God made me!"

"We were told we had to repent and turn away from our ignorance because God had fixed a day when he was going to judge the world through a perfect man," Spiro scratched his head. "I didn't understand that bit," he admitted, "but then Paul said that the proof that this man was God's man was because he had raised him from the dead."

"That's Jesus!" Zak exclaimed.

"But I thought Jesus was the Jewish Messiah," Jules objected. "How come he's suddenly involved in the whole world?"

"Paul says that Jesus came for all people in the world, not just Jews," Spiro explained. "He came to save us by being punished and killed instead of us for all the wrong things we do, and that includes everyone."

"Yes, that's what Moria said," Jules remembered. She rubbed her hand over her eyes, it was all so very confusing. "So anyway, what happened after Paul had finished speaking?" she asked. "Did everyone repent and become followers of this Jesus?"

"Sadly, no," Spiro answered. "When Paul started talking about a man coming back to life after he'd died, some of them just laughed and walked off. But there were others like me who wanted to hear more. My friend Dionysius and a woman called Damaris joined a group of us, and Paul taught us more about Jesus and the Holy Spirit. Even though Paul has gone to Ephesus, we still meet together regularly to learn more."

"Holy Spirit?" Zak asked. "Whatever is that? I don't remember Apollos telling us anything about that."

"Him," Spiro corrected, "the Holy Spirit is a Him. He is the one who helps us understand about Jesus. Without him we wouldn't be able to do anything good."

Jules had heard enough. This whole Jesus thing was getting altogether too complicated she thought. First they say there is only one god and all the gods she worshipped were false. Then they say there's another person called Jesus, who sounded like a god to her. And now they were bringing another god called a Holy Spirit into the story. Was it one or was it three?

For some reason she began to feel quite annoyed. "Come on," she said turning towards the steps, "I think it's time we left. It's beginning to get dark. I'd rather see where I'm going down this hill."

To Jules' relief the conversation turned to more ordinary things once they left Mars Hill. Zak was explaining to Spiro where he needed to go in Corinth and they were working out the best route for the next day's journey.

"We'll take my horse cart," Spiro said. "It's a lot more comfortable than using a mule and we'll get there quicker. It's a great view along the coast road."

When they returned to the house Moria was waiting with another delicious meal. In the centre of the table was a huge fried fish on a bed of green cabbage and in another bowl was a mixed salad with peppers, tomatoes, onions, cucumber and cheese. Fresh vegetables were too expensive for Jules' and Zak's families to afford. This was a real feast.

At last the weary pair settled down to sleep in the main room on makeshift beds that Moria had prepared while they were out. They dropped off to sleep almost before their heads touched the pillows and they didn't stir until they were woken up by Moria and told they should get up ready for the trip to Corinth.

Chapter seventeen

Spiro had been right about the view. As they drove westwards along the scenic coast over the narrow land bridge which connected Athens with Corinth, they could see wide open beaches, secret coves and crystal clear blue waters. With this breath-taking beauty around them Jules thought it wasn't so ridiculous to believe that the mountains and valleys and sea contained godlike beings or mysterious spirits.

"Is Corinth bigger than Athens?" Jules asked.

"Much bigger," Zak replied. "It's about four or five times the size. When I was last there I got quite lost."

"Yes," Spiro agreed, "Corinth is the main government and commercial centre of Greece. You'll find Romans, Greeks and Jews living there. As it has two ports, lots of traders go there to do business, and travellers from all over Greece and Rome pass through. It's especially busy during the Isthmian games, as fans come in their hundreds to stay in Corinth."

Some of the time they travelled in silence as the horse clip-clopped its way along the road, eating up the miles. Jules enjoyed the smell of the eucalyptus trees that grew alongside the track and the sight of cactus plants bursting with yellow flowers. From time to time they stopped for a break and something to eat. It seemed that Spiro couldn't travel too many miles without stopping for food. The friends didn't object either! Moria had prepared such tasty food for them all. No wonder Spiro and Moria were both so plump!

"Not long now," Spiro said, pointing ahead to where they could make out the shapes of grand buildings and temples. "Soon be there!"

In the distance to their left they could see a great lighthouse that guided ships into the harbour. "Look," Spiro said proudly, "those ships have come from all over the world bringing spices from India, silk from China, marble from Turkey and wood from Italy."

The road then swung to the right. In the far distance they could see an imposing hill and between them and the hill was the city of Corinth surrounded by a wall. "That hill is called the Acrocorinth. On the summit there are the ruins of a huge temple to Aphrodite, the goddess of love," Spiro told them. It was an impressive sight.

As they drew closer to the city they could see people putting up tents in the fields on either side of the road. "Who are all these people?" Jules asked in amazement.

"They're getting ready for the athletics," Spiro said. "The games start in a week or so and the fans who want to be sure of a good site will come early to set up their tents. This means the tent makers and repairers will be busy in the city, so we should get a good price for our goods."

"Great!" Zak exclaimed. "How far is it to the market place?"

They were coming nearer to the walls of Corinth and Julianna noticed that the road they were on was paved with marble slabs. "This road is called the Lechaion Way and it leads through the city gates and up to the Roman forum," Spiro answered. "It's not far now."

Sure enough, only a few minutes later they came to the high wall surrounding Corinth. The sharp click of the horse's hoofs on the marble road gradually mingled with the hum of sounds from inside the city. They passed through the great arched gateway and the noises grew louder and louder until they were engulfed in the sounds and smells of people and animals hurrying about their business.

On either side of the road they saw statues of Greek gods. Some of them had been damaged over the years since the Romans had taken over but they could see Hermes with a mountain goat, Aphrodite, and young Palaemon riding on a dolphin. There were statues too of Roman gods that had been built more recently.

"Over there are the remains of the temple of Apollo," Spiro said, pointing to his right, "You can still see some of the columns, but it's in ruins now. It must have been very grand 500 years ago."

"There's the synagogue where Paul preached," Spiro said suddenly. "He was here for eighteen months with Aquila and Priscilla. Their tent shop was just near to here and they did good trade especially during the Isthmian games with wealthy travellers buying new tents. He was thrown out of the synagogue though after a while because of his teaching about Jesus being the Messiah. The Jews got really mad at him."

"In the end," Spiro continued, "Paul told them their blood was on their own heads and from then on he would take the message of Jesus to the Gentiles. He moved into the house of Titius Justus which was next door to the synagogue and carried on preaching there to anyone who wanted to hear. The ruler of the synagogue joined them and that made some of the Jews even more angry. Paul and his friends stuck it out for eighteen months before they moved on. It was hard going but they left behind a huge group of believers—Jews and Greeks—who still meet together regularly."

Chapter eighteen

They were now passing a sparkling fountain and a large impressive pool of white marble which seemed to be fed by a natural spring as the water was crystal clear. "I'd really like to jump into that water," Zak said. "It looks so inviting!"

"That's the Fountain of Peirene," Spiro laughed. "But there's no time for bathing, we're coming into the Roman forum now." As he spoke, the path opened into an enormous market place with shops several storeys high all around.

"There's the shop I need," Zak said and Spiro promptly drew the horse and cart to where he had pointed.

"Stay here," Spiro ordered Jules, jumping down from the cart, "and I'll help Zak with these." She sat, holding the reins of the horse while Spiro helped Zak take his package of woven cloth from the cart. They were gone for a while, but she didn't mind as she was absorbed with looking around her at the grand buildings made of intricately carved marble. All around were shrines and temples to the Roman Emperor and members of his family alongside more Greek and Roman gods. She sighed. There were so many gods. Could any of them heal her father? Maybe none of them had any power.

When Spiro and Zak reappeared from the shop she could see it had been a good sale. Zak was quite red in the face with excitement. "I've sold the lot," he told her, "and I got top prices for every item. My Grandfather will be so pleased."

"He's quite the business man!" Spiro laughed, slapping Zak on the back. "The owner wanted to give a lot less but he held out for the top price. Well done lad. Now let me see if I can do the same with my goods." He paused. "Actually," he said, "I might be a while. Why don't you two explore for an hour or so while I speak to my client?"

"OK, good idea," Zak said, "We'll be back in an hour." And Jules eagerly jumped down from the cart to join him.

"Keep away from that area over there though," Spiro said nodding in the direction of the path leading up to the hill. "See those women hanging around? They call themselves priestesses of the temple of Aphrodite, but if they see you two lads they'll be after your money!"

Zak grinned and handed Spiro his leather purse. "Maybe you should look after my money for me then."

Spiro took it from him tucking it safely under his tunic. "Come on, Jules," Zak said, "I know a good place to bathe."

Jules was glad to be off the cart and able to stretch her legs. Her eye caught sight of a shrine set back from the market place with a huge statue beside it. It was of an old man with a full beard and curly hair, leaning on his staff which had a serpent climbing up it. She recognised the god immediately. It was Asklepios, and her heart jumped as she remembered that he was the god of healing.

"Jules!" Zak shouted. "What are you waiting for?"

Reluctantly Jules turned away and followed Zak. He had found a stream that led into a secluded pool. He had already pulled off his turban and was stripping off his clothes ready to jump into the water. "Come on, join me, Jules," he called. "It's lovely."

Jules felt her face go hot. "No, I don't feel like a swim today," she told him, trying to sound cool, while inside she was trembling. She sat beside the pool and put her hot feet into the water trying to keep calm.

Zak came to the edge where she sat and splashed her with water, grabbing her legs to pull her in beside him. Quickly she pulled her legs away. "I don't want to swim today," she said crossly.

"You're such a girl!" Zak laughed as she moved further from the edge. And he dived under the water, swimming to the other side of the pool before he could see her horrified face.

Julianna gulped. Had he guessed? No, she told herself, it was just an expression. He wouldn't have tried to pull her into the pool if he'd really thought she was a girl. She breathed more easily at this thought.

Chapter nineteen

Zak had lost interest in her now and had found another lad to talk to. She watched him for a moment. Even from a distance he couldn't be confused with anyone else with his hair, now free of its turban, standing up in spikes on his head.

Alone on her side of the pool Jules realised this was her chance. Hastily she gathered up a handful of clay and began making a model. What did lungs look like? she thought, as she moulded the clay into two round balls and joined them together with a thin rolled out piece of clay. She looked at the model she had made. It would have to do.

With another quick glance at Zak she got up, and carrying the clay model with care she walked back towards the shrine of Asklepios.

There were others praying at the shrine when she arrived. She stared up at the face of Asklepios. He seemed to be looking down at her as if he understood. There were many objects laid at his feet; beautiful carvings of an arm, a head, a foot and a finger—all representing the part of the body that needed to be healed.

Jules bent and placed her model of her father's lungs beside them. Would the god even recognise it as lungs?

She bent her head and prayed that Asklepios would have mercy on her father and heal his cough.

When she looked up she saw a man beside the shrine selling small images of Asklepios. Some were beautifully carved in marble, others were made of gold and there were cheaper ones from wood. If only she could afford one of these, then she could pray to him every day.

The man saw her interest and came nearer. "These will make your prayers come true," he urged her. Maybe she could spend some of her money from the sale of the thread on just a small one, she thought, reaching into her purse. But before she could pull out a coin she heard Zak calling her name.

"Whatever are you doing, Jules?" he said as he came up to her.

"Nothing," she muttered, pushing her purse hastily back into her pocket, "just looking."

"Well, stop looking or you'll end up buying something from these crooks," Zak said. "I know these men. They prey on people, making money out of their illness. I know them," he said again, pulling Jules away. "They disgust me. My father is one of them. He knows there's no power in these little shrines, but he gets very rich selling them to ignorant people. I hate him!"

Chapter twenty

It was very late when the tired horse finally arrived back in Athens two days later. Moria was anxiously waiting for them with another big meal which they ate greedily while answering her questions about the trip.

They all agreed it had been a very successful visit and Julianna was pleased that Spiro had also made a good profit on some of the fine thread she had brought and insisted on giving her some extra denarii to take home.

Early the next morning, it was time to say goodbye and begin their return home. Spiro and Moria took them to the dock and made sure they were on the right ship. "Please give our love to your Uncle and Aunt and tell Timon we are praying that he will be healed," Spiro said to Jules, while Moria hugged them both, whispering, "Bless you, my dear," in Julianna's ear.

The voyage back seemed shorter than the trip out. The sea was calm and there was a steady wind that moved the ship along at a good pace. The two friends sat in companionable silence listening to the waves lapping against the sides of the ship as it cut through the water.

There was no shortage of food as Moria had packed their bags full of delicious things—fish, eggs, freshly baked bread, olives, oranges, nuts and dates. "We need to keep eating," Zak said every hour or so. "It wouldn't do to let the food go bad!" "There's no danger of that!" Jules replied, watching as he tucked into his fourth meal of the day.

On the second day the two friends enjoyed watching the numerous ships and galleys that went to and fro on the busy shipping route from Athens to Ephesus. There were small fishing boats that had to avoid getting in the way of the larger vessels and on one occasion they saw a huge galley that Julianna had never seen before.

"Whatever is that ship?" she asked Zak. "See how fast it's going."

"Wow!" Zak agreed. "I've not seen one this close before. It's called a trireme because of the three rows of oars. They're quite old ships and used to be for war but now they're used more for checking grain supplies and fighting pirates. They're fast."

"How many oarsmen are there," Jules asked, "and how do they manage not to clash oars?"

"There are about 170 rowers," Zak answered. "My Grandfather told me about them. They're all tightly packed together in three rows one above the other. They have to practice very hard and all row at the same time."

"Amazing," Jules said and they watched together as the ship sped past them and away into the distant sea.

At last they began to see land in front of them and Julianna's thoughts turned towards home. How was her father? Had he got worse while she was away? Or had Asklepios heard her prayer? Soon she would see her parents again.

Then she remembered. Zak's Grandfather had said he would take her to see her parents on the way home. Her heart sank. What excuse could she give? Could she get him to drop her off somewhere and come back later? No, he would want to take her to the door. Whatever was she going to do?

"You OK, Jules?" Zak suddenly asked, looking at her curiously. "Your face has gone very white."

"Oh," she replied, as casually as she could, "I'm alright. Just tired, I think."

"Well, we're pulling into dock in a few minutes," Zak said. "I'll be glad to get home too. It's been fun though hasn't it? As well as being a successful trip."

Jules agreed. It had been wonderful. If her father hadn't been so ill and she didn't have to pretend she was a boy she would have enjoyed it even more.

"There's Grandfather!" Zak said, pointing out the figure of a man next to a donkey cart.

"How do you know that's him?" Jules asked, peering at the crowd of people and donkey carts waiting on the dock.

Zak laughed. "I can always tell because he's wearing his favourite red shirt. He always wears it when he picks me up after a trip!"

By the time they reached the dock Jules was also able to recognise the cheerful red face and sparkling grey eyes of Zak's Grandfather. Soon they were caught up in the noise and bustle of people gathering up their belongings, all trying to get off the ship before the traders blocked the exit with their huge bags.

"Welcome home, lads!" Grandfather said, helping them both into the cart. "Let's get out of this crowd and then we can talk," and quickly he guided the donkey away from the busy port.

Chapter twenty-one

Jules was glad when Zak began talking non-stop to his Grandfather about the success of the trip and how much profit he had made in Athens and Corinth. As they came to the turning in the road where she had said her parents lived, she held her breath. She shut her eyes pretending to be asleep, praying to whatever god might be listening that neither of them would remember.

"Now Jules," Zak's Grandfather suddenly said and her heart jumped. "What about you?" he asked. "How did your sales go?"

With relief she opened her eyes and saw that they had passed the turning and were moving in the direction towards home. "Oh yes," she replied, "I got good prices for all the thread."

The last part of the ride home they didn't talk much. Zak was nodding off to sleep and Jules was just glad to sit and watch the familiar countryside pass by.

It was good to be home. Zak and his Grandfather didn't stay. They dropped her off outside the house and continued on their way saying, "Grandmother is waiting for us. Goodbye, Jules, give our greetings to your aunt and uncle."

Julianna jumped down from the cart and with a wave and a hasty "thank you" ran inside the house. She was greeted with a cry of joy from her mother. "Oh, how glad we are to see you safely back!" she said, hugging her tightly. She pushed her away to look at her more closely, "You've grown since we last saw you, I'm sure, and you're looking well too. Did you manage to sell all the thread? Is Spiro well? Has Moria been feeding you up?"

Her daughter laughed, "So many questions! But yes to all of them."

"Oh, we've missed you so much!" her mother said, wiping her eyes with the edge of her sleeve. "The house has been empty without you."

Julianna ran to her father's bed. He was propped up and looking more cheerful than she had seen him for a while. "I believe you are looking better!" Julianna cried. "Thanks be to Asklepios! I gave him a model of your lungs and prayed so hard for you to get better and I think he has heard me!"

"No, no, my dear," he answered weakly. "Not Asklepios. I'm better in my soul, but my lungs are still bad. You explain, Lilah," he said as a fit of coughing shook his body.

Lilah smiled gently at her daughter. "Zak's grandparents visited each day you were gone and they told us so many good things. We've learned all about the true God who made the world and about Jesus who came to show us the way." Lilah reached out and grasped Timon's hand. "We are now people of 'The Way'. That's what they call followers of Jesus," she went on. "It has made us both feel so much better."

Julianna turned to look in the corner of the room where the household shrine with all the statues of Greek gods was kept. It had gone. She turned back to her mother with questioning eyes. "We don't need them any more," Lilah said softly. "Now we are trusting in the one true God."

"And do you think he can make father well?" Julianna asked.

"We are praying that he will," her mother replied. "But come now, Julianna, tell us all about your trip. Was it exciting? Did you enjoy the sea crossing? And how are Spiro and Moria?"

"Too many questions all at once!" Julianna laughed. "But look," and she proudly pulled the purse from her pocket and emptied it onto the bed. There was more money there than her parents had hoped for and more than they had seen for many long months.

"Now we can employ a couple more spinners," Lilah said with delight. "You've done so well, Julianna."

"What a wonderful daughter I have," Timon whispered as he looked at the coins spread around him. He reached out and touched her hand, closing his eyes which were full of tears. "Better than any son!" he said.

And that was the best thing that Julianna had heard for a very long time.

Chapter twenty-two

"Your Aunt and Uncle are not the only ones throwing out their household gods," Zak informed Jules next time they met. "There are many people doing the same," he went on. "My father is furious! His business used to be so good and now it's getting more of a struggle to sell his silver souvenirs. Serves him right, if you ask me!"

"This Paul must be quite a preacher," Jules agreed. "The goddess Artemis has been worshipped in Ephesus and all over Asia for years. It's amazing that he has persuaded so many people to reject her."

"Do you want to come and hear Paul?" Zak asked her.

Jules paused. "I'm not sure," she replied, "I've never been into a synagogue, I'm not sure I'd feel very comfortable."

"Oh we don't meet in the synagogue any more," Zak said. "We moved to Tyrannus' lecture hall some time ago. The Jews were saying bad things about Paul and people who were followers of 'The Way' so they decided they couldn't carry on meeting in the synagogue."

"Isn't it expensive to rent that huge place?" Jules asked. She remembered walking past the lecture hall many times and had often wondered what it was like inside.

"Yes, but it's cheaper in the middle of the day when it's hot as none of the other lecturers want to hire it then," Zak replied. "And we need a big place now that we have loads of Greeks as well as Jews wanting to hear about Jesus. Paul does his tent-making work every day while it's cool and after work he goes to the lecture hall and talks and discusses with anyone who goes along. You should come and hear him, Jules."

"Maybe I will, sometime," the girl said vaguely. She didn't tell Zak but she felt very confused. Since she had come back from Athens she had seen the difference in her parents. The worried frown her mother had worn on her face had gone and she seemed much happier. Her father was still coughing as badly as ever but there was a light in his eyes she'd not seen for a long time. Perhaps there was something in this new god Jesus that was different.

Her thoughts were interrupted by the sound of a crowd of people outside a house up ahead. "Wonder what's going on up there?" Zak said.

"Let's go and see," Jules replied.

As they got closer they could see a mad man just inside the doorway of the house surrounded by several Jews. "I know those men," Zak said. "They're the sons of Sceva, the chief priest in the synagogue. I wonder what they're up to."

At that moment one of the priest's sons spoke in a commanding voice, "In the name of Jesus whom Paul preaches, I command you to come out."

"He's trying to cast out the evil spirits," Zak said excitedly. "What's going to happen next?"

They didn't have long to wait to see. A strange voice from the mad man said, "Jesus I know and Paul I know about, but who are you?" Then Zak and Jules watched in horror as the mad man jumped on the other men in a mad frenzy. One man against seven, but he was stronger than them all. He was tearing off the clothes of the priest's sons, beating their bare skin until at last they struggled free and ran out of the house.

In fact, the whole crowd was terrified. They had seen how powerful and dangerous it was to use the name of Jesus. Jules was stunned. "I don't understand," she said turning to Zak. "What actually happened just then?"

Zak shook his head. "I don't know. They were trying to heal the mad man by calling on Jesus, but they don't even believe in Him," he said. "Maybe that was the problem."

All around them people were discussing what had happened. "This Jesus must be a very powerful God," one man said and his friend agreed. "I was doubtful about this Lord Jesus," he told him, "but after seeing this I believe in him now."

"Come on, Jules," Zak said at last, pulling her onto the path. "Your aunt will be wondering where you are, and I'm getting hungry." Silently Jules fell into step beside him and they walked up the path towards home both lost in their own thoughts.

They parted at the usual place at the bend in the path. After Jules had gone a few paces she stopped and turned to call Zak.

"Yes?" he asked.

"I will come and hear Paul," Jules told him. "I think I need to find out more about this Lord Jesus."

Chapter twenty-three

Life had improved a lot, Julianna thought as she sat beside her father trying to encourage him to eat more of the delicious chicken soup her mother had made. Business had been good that morning and she had enough to pay Lois and Dorcas and the three extra workers they had been able to employ since her trip to Athens and Corinth. Also Zak's Grandmother had managed to find them some new customers.

Timon was finding it hard to eat and cough at the same time and after a few mouthfuls he sank back exhausted against his pillow. If only he could be well, Julianna thought sadly. In a short while she was going with Zak to the lecture hall to hear Paul speak. Maybe this Paul had the power to heal him.

Since her parents had decided to become followers of Jesus there was a happier and calmer atmosphere in their home. Zak's grandparents often came to visit and she could see that her father was always glad to see them. She had to be more careful not to be discovered now though, as they could come at any time of the day.

So not only was she a boy outside of the home but she had to be one inside the home too. Sometimes she even forgot she was a girl herself and sat and let her mother wait on her as any son would. Not that her mother minded. "You are working all day like a son, so it's only right that I do all the cooking and cleaning," she would say with a smile when Julianna apologised for not helping.

Julianna carefully filled the spoon with soup and held it up to Timon. "Come on, Father," she said. "Just one more mouthful. Mother made this soup especially for you." She looked at her father's thin, white face and sighed. If only he would get well then everything would be wonderful.

"I think he's had enough, dear," Lilah said gently, taking the bowl from her daughter and laying it on the table beside the bed. "Don't look so sad, child," she said again. "We are all in God's hands, and I feel sure that Jesus will make your father well."

"How will he do that, Mother?" Julianna said. "He's in heaven and we dare not use his name like those priest's sons did. You should have seen them covered in bruises and blood."

"Yes," Lilah replied, "I heard about that from Lois and Dorcas. They say that everyone in Ephesus is talking about it."

At that moment Zak tapped on the door and walked in without waiting for an answer. He was followed by his grandparents. "Zak!" his Grandmother scolded him. "You can't just walk into the house as if you owned it!"

"Sorry," Zak grinned, winking at Julianna who turned quickly away to hide the fact that her face had gone bright red. "I forgot," he said, quite unrepentant, and turned to her parents to wish them good afternoon.

"There's quite a lot happening outside today," Zak's Grandmother said as she sat down thankfully on the bench beside Lilah. "We saw people building a bonfire down the hill and they say that many magicians and sorcerers are going to burn their magic scrolls."

Lilah gasped, "But those scrolls are worth a lot of money, aren't they?"

"Yes," Zak's Grandfather agreed, "they certainly are very valuable and it's amazing that they're not selling them. But they must realise that their power comes from evil spirits and not from the Holy Spirit of God. It is wonderful what God is doing in Ephesus."

"Come on, Jules," Zak said, "If we go now we can see what's going on and still be in time to hear Paul."

"Take plenty of water to drink, Jules," her mother urged her. "It's very hot today. I do hope you enjoy the meeting. Come home and tell us all about it."

Eagerly Jules filled up her water container and soon the two were walking down the path towards the smoke of the bonfire that was coming up from further down the hill.

Chapter twenty-four

There was quite a large group of people around the fire, despite the heat of the day. Zak and Jules joined them and watched as first one, then another, threw large scrolls onto the fire. The magic drawings, recipes for medicines and writings explaining their ancient spells crackled and spat in the fire until they were totally engulfed in the flames.

Jules looked at the faces of the sorcerers and witches lit up by the fire—and by something else that was hard to describe. Joy? Determination? Celebration? She couldn't decide. Some of the people she recognised. Her mother had paid them money for potions and medicines which were supposed to heal her father.

"No more tricks and false miracles from them!" Zak said with satisfaction.

"But they did do real miracles, you know," she told Zak. "I've seen them heal people who couldn't walk and all kinds of things. And they can talk to the spirits of the dead."

"You may be right," Zak replied, "but their power is evil and all kinds of dreadful things happened to people under their spell."

Jules shuddered. "Come on," she said, "I've seen enough of this. I want to hear what your Paul has to say."

The two friends were silent, lost in their own thoughts as they made their way to the lecture hall of Tyrannus. So much was happening in Ephesus it was hard to take it all in. As they approached the lecture hall they could hear singing and Jules looked at Zak in surprise. "What's going on?" she asked.

He laughed. "Oh yes," he said, "since the Holy Spirit has come to us, the people of 'The Way' can't help singing praise to God when they get together."

Jules shook her head in bewilderment as they entered the crowded lecture room. God? Jesus? Holy Spirit? One god or three? And wasn't Paul a god too? People said he was able to do great miracles.

Zak led her to a spot in the hall where they could see the raised platform where a few men stood and she looked around in amazement. The hall itself was spectacular with elaborate drawings covering the walls and beautiful mosaic floors, but it was the crowd that caught her attention. She saw hundreds of people, their faces aglow with joy, singing the most wonderful song that echoed around her, lifting the heaviness from her own heart. Never had she been to a place like this. It was nothing like the temple worship she had seen. This was more real, more holy, somehow more pure. As she looked and listened she felt as if she had entered the gates of heaven itself.

"Is that Paul?" she whispered to Zak as the song ended and a tall, smart man stepped forward on the platform. Zak shook his head. "That's Silas, Paul's friend, the young man behind him is Timothy who's been travelling with Paul and that couple beside him are Aquila and Priscilla. Paul is the little man on the other side of Silas."

The crowd was silent as Silas welcomed them and said a prayer asking God to send his Holy Spirit to help Paul speak clearly about Jesus. The "Amen" echoed round the huge hall and Paul moved to the front.

Jules opened her eyes in surprise as Paul began to speak. She had somehow expected Paul to be a large man with burning eyes and a big voice. This man was a small, rather insignificant man who you wouldn't notice in a crowd, his eyes looked small and weak and his voice was quite ordinary. But the room had gone very quiet now as people listened carefully to all that Paul was saying, and Jules found herself listening too. There was power in his words and it was as if he was speaking just to her.

Afterwards Julianna could hardly remember what Paul had said but she knew that something amazing had happened to her. She knew Jesus was real, that he loved her and had died for her. There was so much she didn't understand but she knew that from now on she would be a follower of Jesus.

"You're very quiet, Jules," Zak said as they walked back at the end of the meeting. "What did you think of the meeting?"

Julianna looked up at him, her eyes shining so brightly that he took a step back. "So," he said, putting his arm round her shoulders, "you have just become a new follower of the Way!"

After a few more steps Zak stopped and picked up a stick. "I want to show you something now," he said, and bent down to draw in the dry soil at their feet. Julianna saw that he had drawn a fish, the same as the one she had seen on the sign outside Spiro and Moria's home. "What does it mean?" she asked.

"It's the ichthus, the sign of the fish. It's a secret sign between people of 'The Way'," Zak explained. "Some people don't like us believing in Jesus, so one way to find out if people you meet believe or not is to draw this sign. I draw one half of the fish and if you are able to draw the other half then I know that you are a follower of Jesus too."

Solemnly Zak drew half a fish in the ground and handed her the stick. With a happy smile Julianna drew the other half and completed the symbol.

Chapter twenty-five

It was a few days later. Zak's grandparents were sitting with Timon when Jules and Zak returned from the market. Lilah was busy cooking and the smell of vegetable stew filled the little house.

How different life was now, Jules thought. There was a peace in her home and in her heart that hadn't ever been there before, even in the days when her father was well.

But the fear of losing her father was still there. She looked at Timon propped up against the pillows, his face pale and thin. He was getting weaker each day and sometimes when he coughed, the cloth held to his mouth was red with blood. "Do you think Paul would come and heal my f ... uncle?" she asked Zak's Grandfather, flushing as she realised she had nearly said "father".

The older man didn't seem to have noticed her slip. "I don't know," he replied, his usually cheerful face looking sad. "It's hard to get anywhere near Paul these days. Wherever he goes there are crowds round him, wanting to hear him preach. There are also quite a lot of protestors around him too trying to stop him preaching. But," he went on, his grey eyes sparkling with determination, "God is doing extraordinary miracles through Paul. The question is how to get Timon to Paul. Leave it with me, Jules, I'll think of something."

Jules smiled gratefully. He would think of something, she was sure. She looked up as her mother put two bowls of stew onto the wooden table across the room and called her and Zak. "Come on, you two," she said. "You've had a busy day at the market, you must be starving." And indeed they were.

As they ate she could hear Zak's Grandfather praying with Timon. When he got to the end she put her spoon down and listened. "In the name of the Father, Son and Holy Spirit, Amen," she heard him say.

There it is again, she thought and jumping up she sat beside Zak's Grandfather. "What does that mean?" she asked. "Are there three Gods or one?"

Zak's Grandfather smiled. "That's a very difficult question," he said. He scratched his head for a minute and then went on, "There is only one God but he is made up of three people—the Father, the Son and the Holy Spirit." Grandfather paused. "I know," he said, when he saw Jules' puzzled face, "it's very hard to understand."

Jules sighed. "It's all very confusing," she said.

"Oh dear," the older man sighed, "I'm not very good at explaining. See if you can do any better, my dear," he said, looking at his wife.

Zak's Grandmother had been sitting quietly listening to the conversation. "Well, let me think," she said. The Father in heaven is the perfect father who cares for us, Jesus is the one who came to take away our sin by dying on the cross and the Holy Spirit is the one who comes to teach us how to live and give us the power to do what is right. So the Father, Son and Holy Spirit are three persons but only ONE God! That's the best I can do, I'm afraid," she said.

"Thank you," Jules said, "it's a bit clearer. Maybe when I'm older I'll understand better."

"I don't think you will," Grandfather said. "Believing it is one thing but understanding the mystery of God is something else! Us weak humans can't expect to be able to understand everything about Him."

"Well, this is all very interesting," Zak interrupted impatiently, "but can I have some more stew, Grandmother? I'm starving!"

She laughed, "And that's something else I'll never understand!" she said, pouring more stew into his bowl. "Where do you put all that food?"

Chapter twenty-six

"Hey Jules! I have a message for you from Grandfather."

Jules was packing up her stall after another busy day at the market when she saw her friend coming towards her. She was surprised to see him. He had never come down to her stall for fear of bumping into his father. The message must be important.

He was alongside her now and he looked excited. "Grandfather says he's been making enquiries and it seems that you don't actually need Paul—you just need one of his old handkerchiefs or aprons."

Jules looked at Zak in amazement. "Whatever are you talking about?" she asked. "What good are old bits of cloth?"

"Sorry," Zak laughed, "I'm not explaining myself. My Grandfather says that handkerchiefs or aprons that have touched Paul are being taken to sick people to heal them!"

"Zak! Is that possible?" Jules asked.

"Well, Grandfather has been talking to a lot of people who say it works."

"Then we must find Paul immediately!" Jules cried, hastily packing up her thread and loading in onto the donkey. Her face was red with excitement. "Where will he be at the moment?"

"At the moment he'll be in front of a large crowd at the lecture hall of Tyrannus. We won't be able to get anywhere near him today. What we need to do is go to his work place in the morning. He works at Aquila and Priscilla's place and it will be easy to pick up a handkerchief that he's been wiping his hands on or mopping his head with. Working in this hot weather makes you sweat."

"You're right! I'll take the day off at the market tomorrow and go first thing. Will you come with me? I'm not quite sure where Aquila and Priscilla's workshop is."

"Of course I'll be there! I know where it is and don't want to miss this!"

Jules beamed with happiness. "At last we have a plan that might work! I can't wait to see him well again. Thank you, Zak, and thank your Grandfather."

More hopeful than she had been for many days she called goodbye to Lucas and turned to leave with Zak.

"Uh-oh, there he is," Zak said quietly looking towards the stall where the man was packing up his silver ornaments.

"There who is?" Jules replied following his eyes. "Oh yes, that's the man who's there every day. He does a really good trade selling his silver wares—although he's not been so busy recently." She looked up at Zak's face which had gone rather white. "Oh, I see," she said slowly. "It's your father."

Zak was already moving up the path away from the market but the man had seen him. "Hey, Zakaria! How are you doing, son?" called the man, and reluctantly Zak turned round and walked slowly back towards the silver covered stall. Jules watched as he spoke with his father for a while. His head was down and she couldn't hear what they were saying. Tactfully she made her way up the path and waited at the well until Zak joined her a few minutes later.

"Sorry, Zak," she said, "I didn't realise he was your father. I've seen him every day. Was it too unpleasant talking to him?"

The boy sighed. "No, it wasn't too bad. I had to meet him sometime, living in the same city." He paused, "Actually it was weird, I found I didn't hate him so much as I used to. In fact, I actually felt quite sorry for him today."

"Why was that, do you think?" the girl asked curiously.

Zak smiled rather sadly. "I blame my Grandmother!" he said. "She keeps praying that the Holy Spirit will help me to forgive him."

"Well," said Jules, "it looks as if her prayer is being answered; which is pretty amazing considering how much you hated him!"

"He was very angry," Zak said, "not with me, but with Paul and Silas. His trade has really dropped off since people have turned away from worshipping Artemis. I didn't tell him I was a follower of Jesus, or he'd have been mad at me too."

"Yes, I suppose it must be hard for traders who sell jewellery and souvenirs for the goddess," Jules agreed. "People take them to the temple to offer them, don't they? But if they're following the true God, they won't be buying them anymore."

"I think there could be trouble brewing," Zak said. "My father says there will be a demonstration tomorrow to protest against Paul's teaching."

"Maybe it's just as well we won't be in the market then," Jules said. "Oh, I can't wait for tomorrow!"

Chapter twenty-seven

Julianna found it hard to sleep that night. She lay awake listening to her father coughing and to her mother encouraging him to take a sip of water. Maybe tomorrow night he would be well and her mother could get a night's sleep. But suppose they couldn't find an apron or piece of cloth? What if she didn't get it to her father in time? And what if it didn't work? By the time the light crept through the narrow window of their little house Julianna was wide awake and ready to go.

"I'm not going to the market today," Julianna told her mother as she struggled to eat her breakfast of egg and bread.

Lilah looked up. "Why not, dear?" she said anxiously. "Aren't you well? You do look very white. A day indoors resting will do you good. You've worked so hard these past weeks."

"I'm fine, Mother. But Zak and I are going to find a handkerchief or apron belonging to Paul. We will bring it home to Father, and he will be well again." She continued in response to her mother's questioning look, "Zak's Grandfather says that many have been healed this way."

"That would be wonderful," Lilah sighed, "but I'm afraid your father is a great deal worse. Last night he was coughing so badly and today he is hardly conscious. If he is going to be healed, it will have to be soon."

Julianna went over to her father's bed. Her mother was right. His skin was grey and his eyes were closed. She could see from his painful gasps that he was struggling to breath and there were blood stains around the pillow where he had been coughing during the night. "Hang on, Father," the girl said urgently. "Please don't die when we are so close to a cure." She planted a kiss on his thin cheek and turned towards the door, her eyes full of tears.

Zak was waiting for her at the brow of the hill where they had first met all those weeks ago. He was looking excited. "What kept you?" he asked. "I've been here hours!" When she didn't reply he looked at her more closely. "You look dreadful," he said. "Your eyes are all red and your face is white."

"He's close to death," Jules explained, "and I didn't sleep too well."

"So let's get going," Zak replied. "We need to walk right to the other end of the market in that direction. Hopefully Paul will be working there today." She followed his pointing finger. Already there were hundreds of tiny figures moving like ants around the square.

"How are we going to get this piece of cloth?" Jules asked anxiously.

"We will get it one way or another," Zak replied determinedly. "But not if we stand here all day. Come on, Jules, let's get going!"

Ten minutes later they were walking down the main road past the civic square and in sight of the commercial market place.

"The market seems noisy today," Jules observed as they moved past the stalls. Lucas was there setting up his stall but Zak's father was nowhere to be seen.

"I suppose he's with the other silversmiths," Zak replied. "They were planning a meeting and demonstration today. I hope they don't cause trouble."

By the time they got to the other side of the market they could see a crowd gathering around one particular man who seemed to be in charge. "Who's that man?" Jules asked.

"I recognise him," Zak replied. "He's one of the leading silversmiths in town; probably one of the richest men in Ephesus. His name is Demetrius. Look, he's standing up to speak."

"Not only in Ephesus but in almost all of Asia this Paul has persuaded and turned away a great many people, saying that gods made with hands are not gods," Demetrius said in a loud angry voice. He was a good speaker and all the other silversmiths were murmuring in agreement.

"There's my father," Zak said, pointing out the man standing at the back of the crowd waving his fist. "Oh dear, he does look angry."

Demetrius was still talking, "There is danger not only that this trade of ours may come into disrepute but also that the temple of the great goddess Artemis may be counted as nothing and that she may even be deposed from her magnificence, she who all Asia and the world worship!"

Jules tugged at Zak's sleeve. "Come on, Zak," she urged. "Remember what we're here for! Where's Aquila and Priscilla's workshop?"

"Just over here," he replied, pulling her towards a large shop set back from the main square on a piece of raised ground. To one side was a pile of tents ready for sale and on the other side were the tools and work bench where the men made the tents.

"Do they all live in that hut?" Jules said in surprise. "I thought Priscilla and Aquila were quite wealthy.

"They are," Zak replied. "Their house is further away in a smarter part of the city. I believe they have a woman and her son who live there and keep their eye on the place. But come on! What are we waiting for?"

Chapter twenty-eight

As they approached the workshop they could see Aquila, Priscilla and Paul but they were not working. Instead, they were standing watching the crowds of silversmiths, their tools and leather spread on the ground at their feet. There were quite a lot of other people standing with them who the friends recognised as other believers in Jesus.

The demonstration was getting louder now and one or two of the silversmiths were shouting out in agreement at Demetrius' speech. One of them shouted, "Great is Artemis of the Ephesians!" and then others took up the chant. People were leaving their stalls to join in and before long the whole market place was in uproar with people shouting in support of the goddess.

Some of Paul's companions had moved closer to the crowd and Paul obviously wanted to get nearer too but some of the believers were trying to hold him back. "This crowd will lynch Paul if they see him," Zak said.

Suddenly some of the silversmiths ran towards the group who had been with Paul and grabbed two of his friends. "They've got Gaius and Aristarchus!" Zak said. "They travelled here with Paul from Macedonia."

"What are they doing with them?" Jules wondered.

"It looks as if they are going towards the theatre," Zak replied. "And so are most of the people in the market by the look of it."

They watched as the mass of shouting people rushed towards the theatre dragging Paul's companions with them. By now Paul's friends had completely surrounded him, and were holding him back from following. It was obvious they were trying to persuade him to leave the market place altogether but it must have been hard for him to see Gaius and Aristarchus in trouble without being with them.

"Zak!" Jules exclaimed. "How are we going to get a handkerchief now? We can't get anywhere near Paul. I can't even see him." She was crying now, with frustration and despair.

Then, just as she was giving up all hope, Zak grabbed her hand. "Look!" he said. At that very moment through the group around Paul they saw him pull a handkerchief from his work apron and wipe it across his eyes and head. "Keep your eyes on that cloth," Zak urged.

Would he throw the cloth onto the ground? But no, he put it neatly back into his apron pocket. Jules stood motionless to see what might happen next. Her heart was beating so hard it was painful. Then they saw him turn away from the workshop with his friends.

"What can we do, Zak?" Jules asked hopelessly. "His friends have persuaded him to return to Aquila and Priscilla's home, and he's leaving and taking his apron with him."

"We'll have to speak to him," Zak said bravely. "Come on, Jules." He grabbed her hand and together they moved towards the workshop hoping that Paul would be sympathetic. He would be worrying about his friends and might have no time for them.

But just then they saw Paul pause, take off his apron and drop it onto a work bench by the hut. Then he and his friends moved quickly away up the hill and out of sight.

The market seemed eerily quiet now. Apart from the shouting coming from the theatre some distance away there were just a few people packing up their wares and loading them onto their donkeys. There would be no business to be had that day.

Jules' and Zak's eyes were fixed on the apron that Paul had dropped. A middle-aged woman began picking up the leather tents and carrying them into the hut. As soon as she went into the hut, Jules leapt forward. Quick as a flash she ran to the apron, reached into the pocket and took out the precious handkerchief still wet from the sweat on Paul's face, and jumped down again to join Zak. She was breathing hard.

"Well done, Jules!" Zak said clapping her on the back. "You make a great thief! Now let's go and give it to your uncle. There is no time to lose."

They were half way across the market when Jules stopped, her face white and anxious. "Maybe it doesn't work if you steal the handkerchief," she said slowly.

"I'm sure it makes no difference," Zak said reassuringly.

"You're right about me being a thief," she continued sadly. "I used to steal grapes every day on my way to the market. That's wrong, I know that now."

"Where are you going?" Zak asked as she turned back towards the workshop, but she didn't answer. "What are you going to do?" he said more quietly.

With a quick step she walked up to the hut where the woman was still packing up the tools. Zak followed behind.

"Excuse me, please," the girl said to the woman who turned and smiled down at her.

"Yes, my lad? how can I help?"

"I'm sorry, but I stole this handkerchief," Jules went on holding up the cloth, her words coming out in a rush. "I took it from Paul's apron. I know I shouldn't have done that, but I really, really need it. You see my f ... that is, my uncle is so ill he is nearly dying."

The woman's smile widened, "That's alright, dear. It happens all the time these days. Take it and you're welcome." She held up her hand as Jules tried to thank her. "But remember, it's not Paul who heals, it's Jesus. Give your uncle the cloth in the name of Jesus. And I will pray he will get well."

Chapter twenty-nine

With a light heart Jules hurried along beside Zak, the handkerchief held tightly in her hand. "You did the right thing, Jules," Zak said and she blushed with pleasure at his approving words.

As they drew closer to the theatre they could hear more clearly the angry shouting coming from inside. "Is there room in there for all those people?" Jules asked.

"Oh yes, and more still. I think it holds 25,000 people when it's full," Zak replied.

"Listen! It sounds pretty bad," he observed. "We've not had a such a riot in Ephesus for as long as I can remember. The Romans clamp down on demonstrations like this."

At one of the entrances to the theatre they saw a crowd of officials discussing what to do. One of them was explaining what had started the riot. "Then they sent Alexander to try to calm the crowd," he said. "He's a Jew and quite high up in the synagogue—but that didn't seem to work. The town clerk has just gone in now. Let's hope he can settle things down. We could get into real trouble with the Romans if he can't."

The noise inside the theatre was much louder now and the crowd were shouting all kinds of different things. "I'm not sure if half of them even know what the demonstration is about," Jules commented.

"You're right," Zak said. "Some of them are shouting 'Great is Artemis of the Ephesians', but I've no idea what the others are shouting. It's a pity we are in a hurry," he continued. "I'd liked to have waited to see what happens."

"Me too," Jules agreed, "but it's very important I get this handkerchief home. Oh Zak, what if he's died during the day? I do hope we're not too late."

They hurried then, only vaguely aware that the noise in the theatre was beginning to quieten. The thought of being too late was unbearable and they half walked and half ran up the hill.

In her haste Jules almost fell into the house when she arrived. Lilah came quickly towards them as they stood in the doorway gasping for breath. "Whatever is the matter?" she asked. "Are you alright? What happened?"

Zak was the first to get his breath back. "We're fine," he said, "but how is Timon? Is he still alive? We have a handkerchief from Paul!"

Lilah sighed. "Only just," she whispered. "He's been so bad today. I don't think he will last very long. You'd best be quick."

Jules ran to her father's bed holding out the handkerchief. She looked back uncertainly at Zak. "Do you think there are special words we're supposed to say? It's important we get it right."

"Grandfather would know," Zak answered. "Should I get him?"

"There is no time," Lilah replied. "Listen." Julianna and Zak bent down over the bed. Timon made a few rasping breaths and then seemed to stop. After what seemed an age he took a few more breaths. “Maybe,” Lilah suggested, “we should say the prayer that Jesus taught. I’ll say it.” And in her gentle voice she began, “Our Father in heaven, hallowed be your name, your kingdom come, your will be done, on earth as it is in heaven ...”

But Julianna could wait no longer. She suddenly remembered what the woman at the workshop had said. Carefully she put the handkerchief on her father’s face and wiped his brow and his mouth. Then she put it over his chest and placed his hand on the top of it and said very loudly, “In Jesus name!”

A silence fell over the little group. Three pairs of eyes stared down at the sick man. Three people held their breath. Lilah was biting her lip so hard that she was drawing blood, and Julianna and Zak found they were holding tight to each other’s hand.

Nothing dramatic happened. There were no trumpets sounding, flashing lights or angels appearing. But the dreadful rasping had been replaced by a gentle, steady breath. His chest was clear; the cough had gone. They watched the lines of pain on Timon’s face disappear and he seemed to have drifted into a deep peaceful sleep.

Lilah and Julianna fell into each other’s arms laughing and crying.

“God be praised!” Lilah cried. “He’s been healed!” while Zak danced around the hut whooping with delight.

“I don’t like to break up your party,” said a quiet voice from the bed, “but I am extremely hungry!”

Chapter thirty

The next few hours were full of activity. Zak insisted on going home to get his grandparents so that they could share in the joy. They came rushing in bringing with them vegetables and meat along with honey cakes to celebrate.

They had such a meal as they hadn't enjoyed for a very long time. Lamb cooked with all kinds of vegetables, followed by fruit and cheese and cakes. Everything tasted especially delicious because Timon was eating with them. Then of course, Timon wanted to know everything that had happened so they talked and talked about all the events leading up to this special day.

"Very well done, Jules and Zak," Grandmother said after they had explained everything. "We're so proud of you both, managing to get that handkerchief when there was so much going on."

"And only just in time, by the look of it," Grandfather said.

"Yes," Lilah agreed, "Timon wouldn't have lasted much longer."

"I was thinking about Paul when I said 'only just in time'," Grandfather said. "I hear he's leaving Ephesus tomorrow."

"Why?" asked Lilah. "He's doing such wonderful work here."

Grandfather nodded, "That's true, but he was never going to stay for ever. His mission is to go all over Greece and Macedonia with the message of Jesus. Once a church is established he moves on. But he's left behind some very good leaders who will continue to teach us."

"So what happened at the theatre?" Zak asked. "Have you heard, Grandfather?"

"Yes," he replied. "Apparently the town clerk managed to calm the crowd."

"How did he do that?" Lilah asked.

"Well, he gave them a good talking to. He pointed out that the men hadn't said anything blasphemous against the goddess Artemis and told them that they wouldn't get anywhere with their unruly behaviour. If they wanted to bring a complaint against Paul or the people of The Way, they should use the courts. Then he dismissed them all and the crowd dispersed. We have a good town clerk you know."

During this conversation Julianna had gone very quiet. She was overjoyed that her father was well again but it was beginning to dawn on her that she would have to become a girl again. There was no doubt about it, she thought, life as a boy was fun. She had known freedom for the first time. Boys had adventures, but girls had to stay at home with their mother. It had been wonderful to wander around the market alone, to be in charge of the market stall and bring money home. She had travelled across the sea and explored places she'd never seen before. But most of all she had enjoyed her friendship and adventures with Zak.

Now it would come to an end. Once he knew she was a girl she wouldn't be allowed to go walking or travelling with Zak. Maybe he would even be annoyed with her for deceiving him, or embarrassed that he had made friends with a girl. It was a dreadful thought. She gave a big sigh which caused Grandmother to stop talking and stand up.

"Come now, we are being very selfish," she said. "Jules and Lilah are exhausted after so many weeks of anxiety. And tonight they will be able to sleep peacefully knowing that Timon is well. We must leave them to rest. It might be best to have the day off work tomorrow. Let things subside a bit in the market."

"OK," Zak said cheerfully. "See you anyway in the morning, Jules! We need to make plans."

"Yes, see you," she replied in a dull voice. But there would be no more plans, she thought sadly, and in the morning you'll probably never want to see me again.

Chapter thirty-one

Next morning Julianna dressed as usual in her boy's clothes. She felt very unhappy as she did so. This would probably be the last time.

"You do need to tell him today, Julianna," Lilah said at breakfast. "I will go over to tell his grandparents at the same time. I hope they understand," she continued anxiously, biting her lip.

"I know I must tell him," the girl replied, "but it won't ever be the same again, will it?"

"No, I'm afraid it won't, but life goes on and you will be able to go with your father to market from time to time," Lilah said.

"And I, for one," Timon laughed, "I am looking forward to seeing my beautiful daughter again." Her father was sitting at the table eating breakfast. It was amazing to see how quickly he had recovered. She smiled happily across the table at him. It was wonderful to see him looking well. He was very thin, of course, but with good food he would soon be back to his old self.

A few minutes later Zak came bouncing into the house. "Good morning, Timon, good morning, Lilah, and good morning, Jules!" he said as he came in. "I've got some eggs here from Grandmother's chicken. They seem to be laying extra at the moment and we thought they would be good for Timon to help build him up."

"Thank you, son," Timon said gratefully, "I do seem to be extraordinarily hungry at the moment."

Zak seemed unusually cheerful, which made Julianna feel even more sad.

"You two go out for a walk," Lilah said. "I'm going to visit your grandparents as I have something to discuss, and Timon needs to have a rest if he is to get his strength up."

Obediently the two friends left the house and went to their favourite spot at the top of the hill where they could look down on the city and out to sea. Silently they watched the bright sails of tiny ships coming into the port and the sparkle of the sun on the waves made by the ships as they moved through the turquoise blue water.

She could put it off no longer. "Zak," she said turning a serious face up to his, "there's something I need to tell you."

"Go on, then," he said, looking down at her with a grin.

"The thing is," her words came out in a rush, "I'm not Jules, I'm Julianna. I'm a girl. Please don't hate me! I had to do it for my father."

Zak threw back his head and laughed loudly. "Oh, is that all? I've known for a long time that you were a girl!"

"What?" Julianna gazed at him wide-eyed in astonishment. "You knew? How?" For some reason she felt annoyed. "I thought I made a good boy," she said crossly.

"Oh yes," Zak went on, more serious now. "At first I was suspicious about your relationship with your parents. I thought you were a boy and until I got to know you a bit I was deceived. But there were things that started to make me think."

"What things?" she asked.

"Well, first there were a few times when you stumbled over Timon's name. I couldn't be sure and I wondered why you stopped yourself calling him something different from Uncle. Then, you never talked about your parents which seemed weird. Also on our way to the port I mentioned visiting your parents and you looked confused and shocked. You obviously didn't want to visit them! It was clear you were hiding something."

"I see that," Julianna said, "but when did you realise I was a girl?"

"That came gradually," Zak explained. "I thought at first you were rather a soft boy. You always tensed up when I sat close to you, which I thought was strange. When we arrived at Spiro and Moria's house, there was that conversation about you being a nephew which made me think a bit more. At that point I was fairly sure you were a girl."

"So why did you try to make me go into the pool in Athens?" Julianna exclaimed. "That was mean! And you called me a girl!"

"I know," Zak grinned. "Sorry," but he didn't look a bit sorry—in fact, Julianna thought he was looking very pleased with himself. "I couldn't help teasing a bit."

"So you don't mind?" Julianna asked.

"Why should I mind?" Zak laughed. "I've never spent so much time with a girl before, and it's been fun!"

"What will your grandparents say?" Julianna asked. "Mother has gone over to tell them this morning. Will they be very shocked?"

"Oh I think they already know," he answered. "They've said things that make me think that they realised. Grandmother has told me on more than one occasion to look after you. And did you notice Grandfather didn't mention visiting your parents when we got back from Athens? I didn't tell them I knew as I thought they might put an end to our friendship and I didn't want that."

"But now it has to come to an end," Julianna said sadly.

"Yes," Zak replied reassuringly, "but not for very long."

"I wish I was a boy," she continued, not really understanding what he meant.

"Well, I don't! I prefer you as a girl!" Zak said, and he wasn't laughing any more. He put a gentle arm around her shoulders. "Because you see," he continued, "in a couple of years or so I'm going to marry you!"

And after that there wasn't much more to be said!